HERBERT CHAPMAN
Football Emperor

STEPHEN STUDD

HERBERT CHAPMAN

Football Emperor

A STUDY IN THE ORIGINS OF MODERN SOCCER

Foreword by Sir Stanley Rous, C.B.E.

PETER OWEN · LONDON

ISBN 0 7206 0581 4

PETER OWEN LIMITED
73 Kenway Road London SW5 0RE

First Published in Great Britain 1981
© Stephen Studd 1981

Printed in Great Britain by
Daedalus Press Somers Road Wisbech Cambs

Contents

Illustrations

Illustrations Nos. 6 and 7, from the *Huddersfield Town AFC Year Book 1925-6,* are reproduced by courtesy of Huddersfield Town Football Club, and Nos. 14, 18, 19 and 20 by courtesy of the BBC Hulton Picture Library.

FOREWORD BY SIR STANLEY ROUS, C.B.E.

I wholeheartedly recommend this book to all football enthusiasts whether they knew Herbert Chapman or not. To those, like myself, who did, it gives an opportunity to relive his brilliant career and to the younger managers, players and football administrators an inspiration to follow the example he set by his enlightened, sportsmanslike and humanitarian contribution to the game of association football.

Chapman was proud of his achievements and all who knew him were proud of him. He played for at least ten clubs – amateur and professional – and became manager of four – Northampton, Leeds, Huddersfield Town and Arsenal. As a player and manager he sought to improve the status of his colleagues, and as a manager proposed improvements to facilities and equipment and strategies. But perhaps his greatest achievement was his ability to win the respect and affection of the players he brought to the clubs he managed. He studied the character of each player, director and colleague, made them happy in their work because he had himself experienced the life-style of each at some time in his career.

Until one knew Herbert he appeared somewhat austere, stern and unapproachable, but when he knew you and his blue eyes twinkled at meeting one felt a warmth and friendliness. He had a lively sense of humour as I discovered one evening after refereeing an Isthmian League match between Tufnell Park and London Caledonian at the North London ground both clubs shared. In the Tufnell Park hotel where we all assembled after the game I heard a voice behind me saying: 'If referees were better performers, the standard of play would improve.' Turning to the speaker in surprise I recognized Herbert Chapman and noticing that he had not shaved that day I retorted: 'If managers shaved before 8 o'clock at night they might get invited to dinner.' (The Isthmian League clubs had a buffet dinner after most matches.) Herbert Chapman replied: 'I will tell you why I

7

haven't shaved today. I had a busy morning and when friends came
to see me I knew, in my unshaven state, they would not invite me to
lunch, and tonight I prefer to go home, so I haven't shaved this evening!' When he wanted to punish the famous Alex James for loss of
form Chapman told him that he was sending him on a cruise to help
him recover his normal good health. Alex arrived at Tilbury expecting to go on board a liner, but a berth had been arranged on a banana
boat which took him only to Bordeaux where he was met and brought
back to England. The lesson was learnt.

I had always admired Herbert Chapman's support for new schemes
and alterations to normal practices. When I was appointed Secretary
of the Football Association I hoped that he would be available to
discuss with me his views on many subjects, but alas like thousands of
others, I mourned his untimely death. During at least two seasons
after his death the players whom he had made into the formidable
team of champions still felt his presence and influence. I remember
after a match at Highbury which the team had won handsomely by
goals by Bastin, Jack and Hulme, congratulating the latter on another
skilful and entertaining display. Joe's reply was: 'We still play for the
Governor, you see.'

There were officials in the game who envied Chapman and sometimes were jealous of his influence. I know of one occasion when
England were playing Italy in Rome and up to half-time were struggling to keep their foreign record intact. There were five Arsenal
players in the England team and Tom Whittaker the trainer. Chapman, thinking a pep talk at the interval might help the players to
improve their tactics, went to their dressing-room. The match ended
luckily in a draw and the member in charge, Mr Kingscott, also
Treasurer of the Football Association, reported this interference to
the selection committee, for which Herbert was mildly rebuked.

Herbert was a family man and particularly proud of his eldest son
Ken who qualified as a solicitor. He wasn't so pleased that he became
a rugby player but would have been proud, if he had lived, to see Ken
elected President of the Rugby Union. In that capacity I met him on
my trips to Twickenham and at Rugby Union dinners to which,
because of my own early connections with rugby clubs, I used to get
invited. Ken reminded me so much of his father – a distinguished
figure of a man sturdily built and full of energy.

The charm of Herbert Chapman's personality still lingers at Highbury. For some years after his death Mrs Chapman was invited to act as hostess to visiting ladies and her daughter Molly still comes to matches from her home in Cornwall. I also see Bob Wall, Herbert's Secretary for years, and former player George Male, and as we meet in the entrance hall at Highbury we turn our faces in reverence to the splendid bust of Herbert who seems to say, 'Keep smiling,' which was his motto in life.

I remember Field-Marshal Lord Montgomery saying to me when I once asked his opinion about a general who had applied for a job at one of the organizations with which I served as Chairman, 'You must be a good picker.' As I read this life story of Herbert Chapman I realize that in all his dealings with players he was a 'good picker'. A reference to the players he engaged at Northampton, Leeds, Huddersfield and Arsenal testifies to this. He looked for character in his men, those who could recognize authority in others while submitting to discipline themselves. He knew the pride and pleasure which resulted from being efficient at one's job. Chapman was delighted when his players were selected for international duty. At least in one match, seven of them. I remember a match in Ireland, when I asked the players to sign their expenses form, all the Arsenal players put 'none' against the appropriate line. They said modestly: 'No expenses, thank you, when we play for England.' It was typical of the amateur attitude which their 'boss' had encouraged.

That friendly outlook still prevails at Highbury. The present Chairman, Denis Hill-Wood, like his father, Sir Samuel, preserves the spirit of friendliness, sportsmanship and high standards of administration and behaviour.

I hope that this book by Stephen Studd will find a place on many bookshelves and be widely read especially by present-day club managers and those who succeed them. If they follow Herbert Chapman's dedication to sport generally and football in particular they too will make a valuable contribution to the welfare of their fellow men.

February 1981   *Stanley Rous*
                                                   President of Arsenal Football Club
                                                   Hon. President of F.I.F.A.
                                                   Hon. Vice-President of the Football
                                                   Association

ACKNOWLEDGEMENTS

The relative scarcity of primary source material on the life of Herbert Chapman greatly enhances my appreciation of the contributions and help I received during the course of my research. In this connection my thanks must go first to Mr Bob Wall, former Arsenal Secretary, now a club director, Mr George Male, former Arsenal and England full-back, and the late Mr Dick Parker, Huddersfield Town director, for talking to me about their memories of Herbert Chapman. The comments of Mr Denis Hill-Wood, the Chairman of Arsenal, Mr Billy Jones, Tottenham Hotspur amateur centre-forward of the 1920s, and the Reverend A. Hunt Cooke were also most useful.

I am grateful for information and material supplied by Arsenal, Grimsby Town, Huddersfield Town, Notts County, and Tottenham Hotspur Football Clubs, and by Mr Kenneth Chapman and Mrs Molly Allsop (Herbert Chapman's son and daughter), Mr Cyril Britten, Mr Harold Whiteley, Mr E. Marsden, Miss Gwendoline Wilkinson, Mrs G. Mallinson, Mr Paul Wain and Mr John Daniels. Letters from Mr T. A. Hartfield, Mrs E. Steeples and Mrs M. Gardiner were also welcome. I am grateful too for the help of the staff at the British Museum Newspaper Library.

I am indebted to Mr Richard Saville and Mr Len Madden for reading the manuscript, offering encouragement and making many useful suggestions, and to Sir Stanley Rous for contributing a Foreword.

Finally, a big thank you to my sister Sheila for her expert typing.

Thanks are due to Messrs Souvenir Press Ltd for permission to quote from *Arsenal from the Heart* by Bob Wall, and to Messrs Weidenfeld & Nicolson Ltd for permission to quote from *Soccer at the Top: My Life in Football* by Sir Matt Busby.

February 1981   *Stephen Studd*

INTRODUCTION

When Brian Clough's Nottingham Forest won the League Championship in 1978, six years after Derby County had won it under the same manager, many commentators were heard to say that Clough had emulated Herbert Chapman in taking two different clubs to the title.

Similarly, when Manchester United's Championship hopes were dashed in 1958, after the club had come top in the two previous seasons, it was said that the Munich air crash had denied Matt Busby the chance of emulating Herbert Chapman's Championship hat-trick.

Such comparisons are inevitable. Herbert Chapman took Huddersfield Town to the top of the table in 1924 and 1925, and the same side was there again the next year, after Chapman had taken over at Arsenal. In 1933 Arsenal were League champions (for the second time) and though Chapman died soon after, it was still basically his team that took the honours for the next two seasons.

Two Championship hat-tricks with two different clubs – an unbeaten record. Not surprising therefore that Herbert Chapman has become a favourite yardstick for measuring the achievements of latter-day football managers.

Arsenal managers in particular, especially during the seventeen years from 1953 when the club failed to gain honours, suffered from the shadow cast by their illustrious predecessor. But as the 1970s saw Arsenal back among the trophy-winners, the comparison became less and less burdensome. When the club carried off the League and Cup Double nearly forty years after Chapman's death, Bertie Mee and his players could at last say they had done as well, if not better, than the legendary manager's team. The phenomenon could have no parallel at any other club. 'Players could

11

then look at the bust of Chapman in the entrance hall at Highbury and say "We've beaten you," ' observes Bob Wall, formerly Chapman's administrative assistant and now a club director. He prefers to put the 1971 Double in an historical context, seeing it as having 'gilded the lily', as if Arsenal, in view of the glories of their past, were somehow destined to accomplish the feat sooner or later.

Yet comparisons with Chapman's achievements go deeper than mere facts and figures. That Herbert Chapman was the first, and probably the greatest, in a line of great football managers is of crucial importance in the development of the game as we know it today.

We are now used to the idea that the fortunes of a football club depend very largely on the calibre of the man in charge, on his ability to recruit the right players, to make the right team changes, to plan effective tactics, to motivate his players. When Terry Venables took over at Crystal Palace, a team renowned as a 'soft touch' suddenly found themselves challenging at the top of the First Division. When Alan Mullery became manager of Brighton, the club entered the soccer élite for the first time in its eighty-year history.

The manager's job entails enormous power and responsibility, and men who cannot use it to bring success cannot expect to last. The post has become notorious for its precariousness, one where only the ablest survive, and in the thirty years since 1945 more than 800 managers have been sacked from or have left their League clubs. Nevertheless, the manager who brings success earns big money and public acclaim. As a proven expert in team planning and management, he is forever in the public eye, regarded as an important mouthpiece both for his club and the game in general, and his views are constantly sought by newspaper reporters and television presenters. His name is included in team line-ups on television as an essential piece of information.

It wasn't always so. In the 1920s the fortunes of a football club were still largely controlled by the chairman and his board of directors. They all had a say in the team make-up – many of them with little or no knowledge of the game. The difference that could be made by having a single 'expert' in charge was first brought to light by Herbert Chapman's outstanding success with Huddersfield

Town. In 1925, as the Town were on their way to winning the League Championship for the second year running, the *Sporting Chronicle* was led to observe:

'No official in football is more attentive to the task of preserving the team spirit than Mr Herbert Chapman, to whom . . . the proud position in football today of the club is in a very considerable measure due. . . . Do clubs realize to the full today the importance of the man who is placed in control? They are ready to pay anything up to £4,000 and £5,000 for the services of a player. Do they attach as much importance to the official who will have charge of the player, who has advised them concerning the choice of this costly talent? . . . . The man behind the scenes who finds players, trains talent, gets the best out of the men at his command is the most important man in the game from the club's point of view.'

Chapman, with his thorough methods and total commitment, was bringing into the game a new kind of professionalism which was to transform it into the highly-organized mass entertainment industry it is today. His life story is largely the story of how English football came of age. Spanning half a century, it begins in a world of roped enclosures, with a game dominated by the amateur spirit even at clubs which had already turned professional. It ends with the marble halls and lush turf of Highbury, with a team attracting huge crowds from London's vast population as Cup and League successes came with astounding regularity.

The Arsenal of the 1930s was the natural and perfect expression of Chapman's professionalism. The team was famous throughout the world, and a visit to Highbury had an appeal to rival the glittering attractions of the fox-trot craze at the dance-halls, or the musical extravaganzas of Busby Berkeley at the new 'super' cinemas. Spectators watched spellbound as the Gunners switched from defence to attack in a matter of seconds, the whole team acting as a single, organic unit with a thrilling and devastating efficiency. Nothing quite like it had ever been seen before.

The style was the culmination of Chapman's theory and practice during twenty years in football management, and was expressive of a new kind of approach to the game, demanding a carefully-planned, scientific method of winning matches. Chapman saw as pitifully outdated the primitive conditions and happy-go-lucky methods of the soccer world he knew as a youth, where the only tactical preparation for a game was a pre-match chat between two forwards, where matches could be played in almost total darkness or be held up because the visiting team had caught the wrong train.

From the time of his first managership, with Northampton Town from 1907, he set about putting the game on a more efficient footing, developing a machine-like tactical system for winning matches, seeing that his players had decent club conditions and were fairly treated as responsible adults, and arranging for more capacious and comfortable spectator accommodation. Later came tactical team discussions and finally, at Arsenal, the first experiments of consequence in floodlighting, numbered players and other novel ideas that are now part and parcel of football.

In the early days, Chapman's revolutionary approach, coupled with an uncanny ability to spot talent and mould players into an effective combination, was already paying dividends. The honours won by Northampton, Leeds City (forerunner of United) and Huddersfield were no less remarkable than those of Arsenal, considering they were usually achieved in the face of economic depression and the predominance of rugby.

Unlike his managerial predecessors and contemporaries, who were under the thumb of the club chairman and directors, Chapman ruled over his creations like an autocrat, and came to be called, aptly enough, the Napoleon of the game. But his régime was not tyrannical – it was based on a deep understanding of his players' individual abilities and problems.

The philosophical distinction has been made between men who are foxes, and know many things, and those who are hedgehogs, who know one great thing. In this sense, Chapman was a hedgehog. Not for him the aimless flow of life's infinite variety, with each new experience valued in itself: everything was subordinate to the one overriding consideration – the achievement of a consistently successful and attractive football team, drawing ever-expanding support and with it fame and fortune.

It was a dream many others must have shared, but no one before him devoted as much energy to its realization. Chapman lived –

and literally died – for it, spending most of his waking hours and probably many a sleepless night in pursuit of his aim, a life-style experienced by all great managers since. For after Chapman, no manager worth his salt could be anything but a hedgehog.

Yet, incredibly, Chapman never meant to be a football manager at all. His appointment at Northampton was intended as a stop-gap measure. Nor was his career one long series of successes. He shone only rarely as a player, and in 1919 was banned from football after being implicated in Leeds City's alleged illegal financial practices. He was soon back, though, to take the soccer world by storm. With an unshakeable, infectious optimism sustained by religious conviction (he was a devout Christian), his reputation took on superhuman proportions.

1

THINGS TO COME

Wembley, Saturday, 26 April, 1930. To the roar of a packed stadium, the teams of Arsenal and Huddersfield Town walked out side by side into the spring sunshine for the eighth Cup final to be staged on the famous turf.

The novel idea of the two teams emerging onto the pitch together came from Herbert Chapman, Arsenal's manager. The teams were led out by their captains, not their managers – that would have been too much of an innovation. For managers, despite Chapman's own fame, were still regarded as shadowy, back-stage figures, of little public interest.

The sight thrilled the Wembley crowd, already treated to a dramatic announcement from Buckingham Palace that King George V, whose visit to the final had been cancelled on doctor's orders, would be coming after all.

For Chapman, aged fifty two, it was a proud moment, a high spot in a career that had already seen great things. For the opposition was almost as much his creation as his own side. It was five years since he left Huddersfield for Arsenal, after taking the Town to a Cup final victory and two League Championships. While he set about team-building at his new club, Huddersfield went on to another Championship and another Cup final, with most of his former players still going strong. Not surprisingly, the Town were now favourites, despite Arsenal's younger average age – 26 years 11 months compared to 28 years 9 months. For Chapman there was no room for sentiment: 'I am a hundred per cent Arsenal now.'

Arsenal started the afternoon at a psychological disadvantage. One of the dressing-rooms had been used by the losers in every Wembley final since the first there in 1923. The Gunners lost the toss, and got the jinx room. But the ever-thoughtful Chapman brought along a gramophone to keep his players' spirits up, and as the machine scratched and hissed its way through lively songs, 'to hear men singing as they dressed was a new feature of football life' (*Daily Mail*).

The game was a classic encounter between two enterprising sides – and the element of surprise added spice to the fare. The biggest surprise came from the Arsenal inside-left Alex James, who, on the coach carrying the team to Wembley, suddenly turned to his colleague on the left, the young Cliff Bastin, and said: 'If we get a free kick in their half, I'll push it out to you. Lay it back to me and I'll have a go at goal.' James was famous for creating scoring chances for other forwards, not for taking them himself, so the rest of the team thought he was joking.

They soon realized that he wasn't. Nineteen minutes after kick-off Arsenal were attacking in the Huddersfield half when they were awarded a free kick. James passed the ball to the wing where Bastin beat the full-back and gave a return pass to James, who let fly with a shot that beat the goalkeeper. 'I imagine there have been fewer efforts more brilliant in a Cup final,' said Chapman of the goal.

Huddersfield kept up the pressure and it was a match full of tension and excitement. 'I was terribly anxious about those danger-laden centres which Smith put across in the second half,' Chapman told the *Sunday Express*. It was not until seven minutes from the end that James laid on a perfect pass for centre-forward Jack Lambert to score Arsenal's second goal. Lambert ran around in the goalmouth clapping his hands, and Arsenal had won the Cup for the first time.

The only shadow cast over the match, apart from the shadow of defeat for Huddersfield, was when the German airship Graf Zeppelin floated over the stadium. The airship, on its way from America, came so low – passengers could be seen waving handkerchiefs from the windows – that it broke the air limit over London of 2,000 feet. Dr Hugo Eckener, the ship's commander, claimed later that he flew low as a salute to the King, after hearing of the Cup final from his British passengers. But that didn't stop complaints from players and some spectators over the temporary loss of sunlight.

Arsenal captain Tom Parker received the Cup from the King, and, in another break with tradition, the Gunners' dressing-room – the jinx broken – was crowded with congratulatory Huddersfield players and their manager, Clem Stephenson, whose career with the Town had begun nearly ten years before when Herbert Chapman signed him as an inside-forward. In the evening, again at Chapman's suggestion, the two clubs set a precedent by dining together at the banquet celebration.

At the civic reception for Arsenal at Islington Town Hall, Chapman dismissed the rumour that he had had a horseshoe in his pocket during the game. 'The Arsenal's success has only been achieved because we showed the team spirit which is necessary to the success of any enterprise,' he announced.

Thus it was that Arsenal, so long in the soccer doldrums, found themselves on the threshold of world fame, worthy successors to those masters of an earlier age, Aston Villa. And it was Chapman who had guided them to this lofty height. When he took over at Arsenal in 1925 he warned in the club programme: 'Do not expect too much in too little time. It will be five years before a major honour is won.' Five years later the FA Cup was on Arsenal's sideboard and a new era in football had begun.

2

FROM COALS TO GOALS

Herbert Chapman, son of John and Emma Chapman, was born on 19 January, 1878 at 17 Kiveton Wales, Kiveton Park, a small mining town half-way between Sheffield and Worksop. He was one of seven children, six boys and a girl.

John Chapman was a coalminer, working long hours in the harsh, back-breaking conditions of the pit. Like many others of his generation and social class, he had no education, and was unable to write even his own name. Sons born into mining communities like Kiveton Park in Victorian times seemed destined to follow their fathers into the colliery that gave the town its living. Such could well have been Herbert Chapman's fate, had it not been for new developments that were to give working-class youngsters opportunities to break out of their social straitjacket. One of these was education; another was the growth of professional football.

The Education Act of 1870, by which the State for the first time assumed a degree of responsibility for the education of all children, made school attendance compulsory up to the age of twelve, the parents paying a small fee of a penny or so a week. So when he was five, Herbert Chapman went to his local school to learn the basic skills of reading, writing and arithmetic, a privilege that his father and millions more like him were never granted.

Both in and out of school sport was the natural outlet for the boys of Kiveton Park, a means of developing personality and self-confidence amid their depressed and depressing surroundings. Chief sports were football in the winter and cricket in the summer, and like most lads of the town, the young Chapman showed early enthusiasm for both. He became captain and secretary of the school football eleven and played alongside his brothers in the local junior team.

But when it came to earning a living, it was coals, not goals, that mattered. His schooldays over, Chapman started to work his apprenticeship at the local colliery. It was not the end of his education, however. In the wake of the 1870 Education Act came a widespread growth in further education, with school boards offering technical courses to children above school age, and Chapman spent much of his spare time studying for a certificate in colliery management. Technical colleges, many of them forerunners of today's provincial universities, were springing up all over the country, and it was at one of these, Sheffield Technical College, that Chapman took a course in mining engineering. He was thus part of a new, literate working class, one of a generation that was to have such a profound effect on English politics and society in the early twentieth century.

Alongside his technical studies went football. He played as an amateur for local clubs, and his passion for the game was shared by most of the working population in and around Sheffield, among them his younger brother Harry, who was to make his name as a professional. For Sheffield was a power-house of football, generating intense local pride and rivalry. Various clubs grew up there in the mid-Victorian period under the aegis of the Sheffield Association. The Association was set up after the original Sheffield club failed to gain admittance to the London-based Football Association, formed in 1863, because of different interpretations of the rules. After 1868, regular games between the two cities created the need for some uniformity in the rules. From its independent position, Sheffield was able to exert pressure on the FA to introduce the tape across the top of the goal posts (nets were not used until the 1890s), and to revise the rules for goal kicks and corner kicks according to the Sheffield code. Although the local rules were eroded in the late 1870s by increasing pressures for national uniformity, Sheffield had nevertheless stamped itself as a vital force in the association game, and it was appropriate that the first experiment in floodlit football should be held in the steel city in the very year of Chapman's birth.

On the evening of 14 October, 1878, the autumn gloom was broken by artificial light coming from the football pitch at Bramall

Lane. The light, from two lamps in each corner of the ground, was generated by two dynamos stationed behind the goals and the brightness of each lamp was equivalent to that of 8,000 candles. Such was the novelty that an estimated crowd of nearly 20,000 came to watch the match, between two local sides, in a year when the Cup final was watched by 5,000. Official attendance was put at 12,000, but at least another 7,000 got in without paying. The team captains were brothers, W. E. Clegg, later Sir William Clegg, Lord Mayor of Sheffield, and J. C. Clegg, later Sir Charles Clegg, President of the Football Association.

Football at this time was entirely an amateur game. Clubs were formed first by 'old boys' from the public schools (such as the Wanderers and Old Etonians), then by churches (Southampton, Queen's Park Rangers), factory workers (Arsenal, West Ham United) and cricket clubs (Tottenham Hotspur). The competition for the FA Cup, instituted in 1872, was dominated by the amateur pioneers the Wanderers, who won the trophy five times in the 1870s, the Old Etonians, Oxford University and the Royal Engineers.

The Royal Engineers of Chatham, organized by Major Francis Marindin, joined the FA in 1869 and were the first recorded team to demonstrate the importance of fitness and team spirit. They played the then customary tactical formation of one full-back, two half-backs and seven forwards, but put emphasis on the combination as opposed to the mere collection of individual talent, and showed the value of passing skills as opposed to the prevalent art of dribbling. Tony Pawson, in his *100 Years of the FA Cup*, writes of the 'Sappers':

'The Sheffield Association, who had many splendid games with them despite the initial difference in their rules, noted their ability to be all up in attack or back in defence. They were fit and fast enough to have the whole team covering the goalkeeper one moment, then surging up-field the next.'[1]

The amateur game was gradually undermined as football took hold in the industrial cities of the North and Scottish players came from across the Border in search of work. J. J. Lang, who joined Sheffield Wednesday from Glasgow Eastern in 1876, is thought to have been the first professional, but it was Lancashire that was to lead the way in developing the professional game, after Jimmie Love and Fergie Suter joined Darwen from Partick in 1878. At a time when payment of players was still prohibited, Blackburn Rovers became a fully professional team, winning the FA Cup in three successive years from 1884. Preston North End then Aston Villa followed them as the outstanding clubs of their time, winning the Cup and League Double in 1889 and 1897 respectively. Despite attempts first to stamp out payment to players then to limit it, professionalism spread rapidly, wresting control of the Cup from the established amateur sides, and was legalized in 1885. Final recognition came when the separate Amateur Cup was introduced in 1893. By that time there were more than 1,000 professional players registered with the English Association. At first their wages varied from 2s 6d to 30s a week, plus bonuses, and it was not until 1901 that a maximum wage, £4 a week, was set.

With the decline of the amateur and the growing incidence of crowd violence at matches, soccer began to be frowned upon by 'respectable' society. Nevertheless to a young man of working-class origins, seeking to avoid having to go down a mine for a living, professional football was an obvious and attractive way out. Herbert Chapman may well have considered this, but at this stage he still saw his future in mining technology and retained his amateur status even while playing for professional clubs. Though he did later turn professional he said, looking back, that if he had his time over again, 'I should prefer to remain an amateur. I do not believe any man would choose to be a professional if the question of earning a living did not arise.' [2] He remained loyal to the concept of 'pure' football, as a thing of value in itself, without the demands of success, the scramble for major honours, the non-sporting trappings of big money.

In 1897, after playing for various clubs in Sheffield, Chapman moved further afield, across the Pennines, to Stalybridge Rovers, a Lancashire League club whose chief claim to fame was the regular loss of its footballs in the nearby River Tame during home matches.

By this time association football had already assumed many of the features familiar to modern spectators. A league system, dom-

inated in those early years by the northern clubs, was established in
1888 to provide regular fixtures for professional clubs. A Second
Division was created in 1892 and a promotion and relegation
system in 1898. Clubs in the South formed their own Southern
League in 1894.

Originally, two umpires controlled the game, with a referee to
decide points of difference between them, but in 1891 the referee
was given sole charge while the umpires were converted to linesmen. In the same year the penalty kick was introduced and goal
nets made compulsory, while the practice of changing sides after a
goal was scored had already been abandoned in favour of the
change at half-time. The referee's whistle, introduced by Nottingham Forest, had replaced the white flag used earlier.

Other features of the modern game were slower to make their
appearance. Players' knees were modestly covered by their 'shorts',
they wore no numbers on their backs, and covered accommodation
for spectators was a rarity at all but the biggest clubs. Substitutes
were not allowed. Formations were relatively simple, without
the sophistications of late-twentieth-century soccer. Nottingham
Forest, who also invented shin-guards, were the first to use the
system of two backs, three half-backs and five forwards, two paired
on each wing, and the formation became standard after Accrington
Stanley adopted it in 1893.

The offside law then in force ruled that a player was offside if
there were not at least three opponents between him and the opponents' goal when the ball was last played.

From Stalybridge, the nineteen-year-old Chapman launched
himself on a chequered career as an amateur inside-right, travelling
around the country and lodging wherever there was a team place
and a job. He was to find everywhere the casual organization and
easy-going attitudes that characterized the local clubs he had already played for. Rochdale, for whom Chapman made his first appearance on 16 October, 1897, were probably typical. They were
drawn at home to Horwich in the second qualifying round of the
Cup, but the local athletic ground, used by the club, had prior
booking for a hurdle race. So the tie was held at Horwich, where
Chapman made a favourable impression in a 1–1 draw. Two weeks

later he scored his first goal for Rochdale, against Ashton North End.

Late arrival at away matches of players left to make their own way there was a common hazard for clubs, as Chapman himself found when Rochdale were away to Bacup in November: he missed his train connection and arrived forty minutes after the kick-off. To make matters worse, the Rochdale captain had to leave the field soon after with an injury and, with ten men for much of the game, the team were lucky to lose by only 3–2.

At the end of the season, Chapman moved on to Grimsby, signing amateur forms for the Town in May 1898. It was a bad time for Second Division Grimsby. They had just had their worst season since joining the League, and were in the grip of a managerial crisis that was to provide Chapman with many valuable lessons for the future.

Like many other clubs of the time, Grimsby was managed by a committee, with no one man responsible for the running of the team. Relations with the players grew so bad that indifference and indiscipline made training sessions a nightmare for the trainers. Other, more successful clubs had already adopted the idea of having one secretary-manager dealing with day-to-day affairs under the overall control of the board, and such a post came to be mooted at Grimsby. 'Experience', the *Grimsby Gazette*'s football columnist, pointed out that a man capable of carrying out the functions of a secretary-manager 'could not be obtained under £150 per annum' and that this was beyond the club's means. He recommended instead a system whereby the existing secretary would take charge of the team under orders from a much-pruned management committee of three. He also called for a 'better and healthier spirit among the players' to be secured by a closer relationship between players and management, instead of the existing situation where a player met his bosses only when he was being reprimanded for some misdemeanour.

Chapman did his best to counter the evils of ineffective management by working out tactical moves with Greenwood, his partner on the forward right. The *Grimsby Times* reported that the pair 'set an example of understanding and teamwork' that was not matched by their colleagues. Indeed any planning of tactics had to be done by the players themselves, even at the biggest clubs, where management – the directors and their officials – concerned themselves chiefly with finances and selection of the team.

At Newcastle United, for instance, one of the outstanding teams of the 1900s, the players held their own tactical discussions and defender Billy McCracken perfected the offside trap to an infamous degree. On one occasion the chairman even told three of the players to lock themselves in a room and work out the best team. But clubs were lucky to have such players. As late as 1914, senior official and former referee John Lewis commented: 'It is certainly true that our professionals evince no great anxiety to learn anything of the theory of the sport and that in most teams there is no evidence of pre-conceived tactics or thought-out manoeuvres.' [3]

At Grimsby, Chapman was popular for his dash and energy, though he lacked steadiness in front of goal. 'If on the small side,' said the *Grimsby Gazette*, he was nevertheless 'sturdily built and takes a lot of knocking off the ball.' Boxing Day 1898 saw something of a family reunion at Grimsby when Chapman's brother Harry, also an inside-forward and playing for Worksop, was given a trial. Harry's brilliance as a player cast a shadow over his elder brother which lengthened as the years wore on.

Life as an amateur footballer was hard but rewarding. Chapman made many friends, in the team and at church on Sunday, but his social life was severely limited by work and study. He had to take any job going (one was in a print works) and, whatever the job, working hours were long and wages low. He spent most of his evenings poring over engineering textbooks by the light of an oil lamp. He lived frugally, and learned to make a little go a long way.

After a poor performance at centre-forward, a position which never suited him, Chapman was dropped from the Grimsby team. Before long he was travelling west, to sign as an amateur for Swindon Town. Bob Menham, the Town's goalkeeper, remembered the new man as the Rochdale forward who put three past him in a Christmas match when he was keeping goal for Wigan. Chapman scored both goals in a 2–0 win over Chatham in October 1899 and was described by the *Swindon Advertiser* as an effective tackler, creating openings for goal, but having a 'tendency to ramble'. Nevertheless, Chapman did not stay long in Swindon. He found jobs hard to come by (despite the Great Western Railway engineering works being based in the town) and in November he was off again, to play for the Kent club Sheppey United.

The 1899–1900 season was overshadowed by the Boer War, and attendances were down. It was a particularly disastrous season for Sheppey. Although they won the Chatham Charity Cup, they were relegated to the Second Division of the Southern League. Chapman was probably one of their best players during his three months there, maintaining a consistent goal-scoring form, possibly the best of his amateur career. Early in February 1900 he distinguished himself by scoring the first goal from a corner kick seen at the Botany Road ground that season – against Tottenham Hotspur – and the next week scored in the opening minute of a Charity Cup match at Gravesend.

He left Sheppey on a note of heroism. He was injured in a rugged home encounter with his previous club Swindon on 3 March. While he was attended to in the pavilion, Sheppey's men battled on, but were soon 4–1 down. Chapman insisted on returning to the field to put matters right, and was greeted with admiring cheers. But he had to go off again – this time for good. Nursing his wound, he packed his bags and headed north.

It was to his home city of Sheffield that the wanderer returned, and there he took up his mining studies in earnest. As the summer of 1900 drew to a close, however, football fever renewed its hold, and he accepted an invitation to play for nearby Worksop, newcomers to the Midland League. Playing mainly for the reserves, he scored a hat-trick against Derby County reserves and by the end of the season was second highest scorer with eleven goals in twenty-six appearances. Most of those goals came in early matches, however, and as the season wore on his form deserted him. In contrast, Harry, the brightest footballing star of the Chapman family, was about to launch himself on a distinguished career as a brilliant, sharp-shooting forward with Sheffield Wednesday, who were to go on to win the League Championship in 1903 and 1904, and the Cup in

1907. Harry Chapman was given a trial with Wednesday in February 1901, and from then on, as a player, Herbert was to be completely eclipsed by his brother's fame.

In February too, all football was banned for two weeks as part of national mourning at the death of Queen Victoria. The Football Association postponed its Cup ties for a month 'to give expression to the profound grief which is felt by its members on account of the death of Her Majesty', and the *Worksop Guardian* painted a somewhat idealistic, almost tribal, picture of local footballers who 'stood in doorways and met over fires to discuss prospects and the new King'. A new era was dawning, one in which profound changes were to take place in most walks of life, including football.

3

NORTHAMPTON AND BACK

Some time during 1901, Herbert Chapman decided to try his luck as a professional footballer. It is not known for certain why he took the plunge, but the move was probably well judged, for the twenty-three-year-old was serious-minded enough to work out the pros and cons. He probably felt sufficiently assured, with his qualifications, of a future in mining engineering, once his playing days were over – and he later came to admire players shrewd enough to look after their own best interests in this way. For players who did not make early arrangements for when they retired from the game faced the obscurity and poverty of the unskilled labourer.

Chapman turned professional with the club he was so soon – and so unexpectedly – to manage. Northampton Town was formed in 1897 and four years later joined the Southern League as a fully professional side. After Chapman played against them for Worksop, Northampton's president Pat Darnell invited him to join them. The player accepted and after a summer of playing and acting as secretary for Kiveton Park Colliery Cricket Club, Chapman left home again, to meet new friends who were to alter the course of his life.

He turned in some creditable performances for Northampton, including two goals against Cup-holders Spurs in October 1901. But the season was not without its disasters, notably an 11–0 defeat at Southampton just after Christmas, which showed how costly the lack of proper organization and forethought could be. After a gruelling journey in a stopping train from Waterloo, the team arrived at the Dell just in time for the kick-off, only to find that, while they had brought boots for hard, frosty pitches, Southampton's ground was muddy.

Chapman's full-time commitment to the game came at a

time when soccer was cementing its status as the national sport.
Football's enormous growth in popularity was reflected in Cup-
final attendances, which rose steadily from a mere 2,000 for the
first final, at the Oval in 1872, to nearly 111,000 at Crystal Palace
in 1901, when Tottenham became the first southern club to take
the trophy. And the association game was beginning to make in-
roads on the Continent too, where it was introduced by visiting
English teams at the end of the nineteenth century. Football
associations were formed in the Netherlands (1889), Italy (1898),
Germany (1900), Sweden (1904) and Spain (1905). Austria
played Hungary (both part of the Habsburg Empire) in the first
international match in Europe in 1902 (Austria won 5–0), and
England's first game with a foreign side was against Austria in
Vienna in 1908.

At home vast crowds, enjoying the recently-introduced Saturday
half-holiday, flocked to football grounds all over the country every
weekend to watch stars like Billy Meredith, Manchester City's
'Prince of Wingers', 'Happy' Harry Hampton of Aston Villa, and
Sheffield United's Ernest 'Nudger' Needham, the small, energetic
midfield player. Needham was part of the smallest half-back line
ever to win the League Championship, when Sheffield United
took the title in 1898 (all three half-backs were under five feet six).
With skipper Needham the inspiration of their play, United were
one of the most successful sides of the period, winning the Championship and making three Cup-final appearances in the years
1898–1902. It was they who lost to Spurs in that 1901 final (in a
replay), but the following year they took the trophy for the second
time. And it was in that 1901–2 campaign that Chapman played
against them for his new club.

Cup fever hit Northampton on 25 January, 1902, after the
Town had survived the qualifying rounds for the first time to earn
a home draw with Sheffield. It was Northampton's big day, and
barriers were put up round the pitch to stop encroachment by the
expected large crowd. The local Press noted that women were
showing great interest in the tie, and a minor controversy blew up
over whether ladies should have to pay the full admission price of
6d to undergo the hardships of the terraces with the 'sterner sex'.

The club itself was in no doubt: women may not have had the vote, but sexual equality at the turnstile was the order of the day.

Interest in football among women was not, in fact, uncommon, and there were several women's clubs formed in the 1890s, notably at Preston.

Chapman, at twelve stone nine the heaviest member of Northampton's team, played well against a side that included Alf Common, later to become the first £1,000 footballer, and the irrepressible Needham. But Sheffield won 2–0. Needham congratulated Chapman on his performance after the game, and proof of his admiration came at the end of the season when Sheffield United asked Chapman to play for them. Chapman agreed on condition that he could resume amateur status. Having got his diploma from the Institute of Mining Engineers, he wanted to gain practical experience as a mining official. This was settled, and Chapman set out once again for Sheffield.

Sadly, however, it was soon obvious that his playing skill was beginning to wane. One of his best games for United was against Liverpool in November 1902, when he was, according to the *Sheffield Daily Telegraph*, 'both fast and smart' in a 2–0 win, but he soon faded from the scene. Notts County showed an interest in his bustling style of play, being impressed, they said, by his habit of taking the shortest and most direct route to goal. In May 1903 they signed him, on professional terms, for £300.

The 'Brother of Chapman of Sheffield Wednesday' did not make a happy start: he was dropped after his first game. This was typical of the management at Notts County. The team as a whole suffered from constant shake-ups and Chapman was to retain a lasting impression of the way morale was destroyed by this re-shuffling.

The Notts forwards were almost bottom of the First Division list for goals scored while the defence shared top place for goals conceded. A campaign against this mismanagement by the club directors was waged by the *Nottingham Daily Express*, which was especially critical when Chapman, 'the only dangerous forward on the field', was dropped. But in March 1904 even he lost favour and was dismissed as 'too clumsy' for a forward.

At the season's close the captain, Walter Bull, who had been with

the club for nine years, left for Tottenham, where he was later
to be instrumental in launching Chapman on his managerial career.
At the same time, Chapman returned to Northampton. He had
made too many friends there to stay away for long and when, in
March 1904, a Notts team visited the Cobblers for a friendly
match Chapman had been able to look up some of his old acquaint-
ances. Earlier, in November 1903, it had even been rumoured that
he was to be transferred to Northampton in an exchange deal.

Apart from two short periods of injury, Chapman held a regular
place with Northampton throughout the autumn and winter of
1904–5, often at centre-forward, not usually his best position. His
popularity at Northampton was fanned by his podgy physique, and
once there was much laughter on the terraces when he rolled into
the net like a ball after missing a cross from the wing.

His form at length caught the attention of Southern Leaguers
Tottenham, who signed him in March 1905 for £70, to fill the gap
left by the untimely death of their inside-forward, Jones. He scored
in his first game for Spurs, against Brighton, but thereafter his form
once again deserted him, and supporters were angry when he was
retained at the end of the season.

Chapman spent the summer playing for Spurs' cricket team, and
early in the new football season won over supporters with a spark-
ling display of shooting and passing, and headers which brought
two goals against Reading. 'Chapman's a Dasher,' said the cartoon
in the *Tottenham Herald*'s Spurs feature that week.

After a match on 10 September, Chapman, now twenty-seven,
travelled to the Midlands to fulfil a more personal engagement. In
the Nottinghamshire village of Annesley he married Annie Poxon,
whom he had met back home in Kiveton Park, where she was
teaching. The couple set up house in North London, and the new
Mrs Chapman resumed her teaching career there – sparking off
a local controversy in the process. The battle for women's rights was
in its infancy, and it was still regarded as somehow immoral for
married women to teach. On 7 November, 1905, it was proposed at
a meeting of the Edmonton Education Committee that the post at
Silver Street School which Mrs Chapman held on supply should
be advertised, because her husband was earning £4 a week as a

footballer and 'he surely ought to be in a position to keep her at home'.

Against this it was argued that a footballer's wages did not provide security as a player's career was short-lived. The common-sense argument – that she was good at her job – finally won the day after the headmistress reported that Mrs Chapman was 'an efficient and up-to-date teacher and disciplinarian' whose class had improved in every way. Mrs Chapman held her post – but only by a single vote.

Chapman, meanwhile, continued to build on his new-found form. He scored twice against West Ham, getting a black eye from a full-back in the process. He was injured in the mouth against Plymouth Argyle and had to carry a sponge around the field with him to bathe the wound. The game at Plymouth was also notable for a strange decision by the referee. After the Argyle goalkeeper had collected the ball, Chapman got hold of him and swung him round over the line. The result: a corner!

With the Cup campaign came training at the seaside. A change of air in the week before a Cup tie had become common practice at professional clubs ever since Blackburn Olympic had taken its team to Blackpool in 1882, and was symptomatic of the change from amateurism. In both 1906 and 1907, Chapman travelled with the Spurs to Leigh-on-Sea. Training was at the Southend Kursaal, where the players enjoyed hot sea-water baths, said to have a 'wonderfully stimulating effect'. But Chapman's appearances for the Tottenham first team grew scarcer as his form deserted him again. The *Tottenham Herald* commented that Chapman 'began by getting goals with a fair amount of frequency, but for some time past he has been no better than the others in this respect.' His appearance as 'a stylish, if not vigorous, batsman' in the players *v.* officials cricket match in the summer of 1906 was a pleasant contrast.

His days at Tottenham were numbered when Spurs went out of the Cup at Notts County in February 1907, his inclusion in the side arousing widespread criticism. He had relapsed into that mediocrity for which, as a player, he was to be chiefly remembered. In his character, however, he still showed that youthful zest which he was

1 Herbert Chapman in 1933.

2 Chapman (sitting, left) as a player with Notts County, 1904.

3 Chapman (sitting, second from left) in the Spurs squad of 1905-6.

to retain throughout his life. A stocky man, with a round, friendly face, piercing blue eyes and a broad smile, he seemed the very embodiment of self-confidence as he stood before the camera at White Hart Lane in his Spurs strip, feet astride and arms folded, like a man fresh from victory and ready to dash off at a moment's notice to score more goals for his side. The reality, however, did not match the appearance. The playing career that was drawing to a close had been undistinguished, punctuated by the occasional flash of brilliance. Nevertheless, for the future it was to prove an invaluable experience. Chapman had travelled widely, his longest period with any one club being two years with Spurs, where he had got to know North London, then without the Arsenal. He knew many football centres throughout the country, large and small, and had seen at first hand the strengths and weaknesses of a wide variety of teams, styles and tactics, noting the effect on them that management could have. These experiences were to prove more valuable than he could have realized. For his career was about to take a sudden and dramatic turn.

In the spring of 1907 he received an SOS from his old friends at Northampton. The Town had dropped to the bottom of the Southern League's First Division and support was falling away disastrously. Their secretary-manager had been sacked and the club asked Chapman to persuade his Spurs and former Notts County colleague Walter Bull to take over, as he was about to give up playing. Chapman duly obliged and the matter seemed settled.

Lying in the bath at White Hart Lane after a game at the end of March, Chapman looked back contentedly over his own playing career, also drawing to a close. Whatever his faults as a player, he had enjoyed every minute on the field, revelling in the challenge of finding a way through the most dogged defences. Now he looked forward to a secure future in mining armed with his diploma and work experience. But his reverie was interrupted by Walter Bull, who strode into the bathroom and told him that he had decided after all to stay on at Tottenham for another year, so wouldn't be taking the Northampton job. 'Why don't you take my place?' he suggested. 'It's more in your line.' Chapman considered the idea as he dressed. After talking things over with his wife, he sat down to write to the Northampton directors putting himself forward as player-manager – on a temporary basis, as he still wanted to be a mining engineer.

His offer was accepted by Northampton, after they failed to get former Stoke and Manchester City half-back Sam Ashworth for the post.

The appointment, made on 9 April, 1907, required the consent of the Spurs directors, as Chapman's contract did not run out until two days later, when he played his last game for Tottenham, a 2–0 win over Queen's Park Rangers at White Hart Lane. On his departure the *Tottenham Herald* commented: 'Although we can hardly say that he is in the first flight of footballers, he is a most conscientious player and a gentleman both on and the field.'

4

THE FIRST TITLE

One result of the growing professionalism and popularity of soccer in the late nineteenth century was the formation of football clubs as limited companies. Clubs began life run by committees of unlimited liability, but as the financial turnover increased with payment of wages, costs of travel to away matches and ground maintenance, and dependence on gate money for revenue, the risks involved compelled them to adopt limited liability as public companies. And as public companies, clubs gained an extra source of income in the sale of shares. Most League clubs assumed this status towards the turn of the century, replacing their committees with boards of directors – mostly local businessmen and dignitaries – so that today all League clubs are limited companies except Nottingham Forest, which is still run by a committee.

Northampton Town, formed in 1897, became a limited company in 1901 when they joined the Southern League. Their president, like the chairmen of most other clubs of the time, played a key role in directing affairs, securing players and choosing the team, while the secretary-manager, as a mere employee, played a subsidiary, administrative role. Just as men like Major Sudell, Preston's chairman, and Aston Villa's financial secretary F. W. Rinder were the main driving force behind their clubs' fortunes, so Pat Darnell, who had first brought Chapman to Northampton, played a leading part in club and team policy.

Yet soon after Chapman took over as manager, there was no doubt as to who was responsible for early successes. The *Northampton Daily Reporter* wrote of 'the popularity which manager Chapman's team has quickly gained', of the manager's 'businesslike methods' and his natural ability to inspire confidence and of 'a general belief in the capability of the Cobblers' new team'.

In less than two months of Chapman's first season as manager Northampton were proving themselves a vastly improved side, winning back support from a public disaffected by the poor showings of the recent past. In April 1907 the *Daily Reporter* had called the fixture between New Brompton and Crystal Palace, on the last day of the season, a match 'to decide which team is nearly as bad as Northampton'. The mere arrival of Chapman as player-manager pulled back the crowds, to whom he was still something of a hero. Gate receipts of £67 for the first game of the new season were seen as a great improvement – an indication of the poor state the club was in previously. (Even if everyone paid the minimum admission charge of 6d, the maximum crowd would have been only 2,680.) The Cobblers, with Chapman at inside-right, took the field against Plymouth Argyle wearing smart new jerseys, as if to underline their faith in a new era. But they had to change in the cricket pavilion (Northampton still shares its ground with the County Cricket Club), as alterations were being made to the dressing-rooms.

Northampton lost this opening game, but subsequent victories stamped them as the most improved side in the country. The *Reporter* called a 2–0 home win over Millwall in October 'a display of fast football' of 'real skill and polish', and commented: 'We have had no football like this from a Town team for many moons.' Before long Northampton were being tipped for the Southern League Championship.

But the job of hauling Northampton from the bottom of the table had not been without complications. In the summer Chapman was immediately faced with something of an Edwardian George Best affair – the Town's goalkeeper Cooch disappeared. His contract for next season had been agreed, but letters sent to him were not answered. The disappearance appears to have been a rebellion over pay, a protest at not being able to earn more than £4 a week. As a *Reporter* reader expressed it:

> Some say it's all a bit of bluff,
> That Cooch is only in the huff,
> Not being offered quite enough
> Of screw to stay.

One rumour had it that Cooch had gone to Scotland, to replace Dundee's goalkeeper, who was leaving. But on 3 May the
dissident returned.

Chapman then set about getting new players. At centre-forward
came Fred Lessons, 23, who had spent three seasons with Nottingham Forest and played for them in their tour of Argentina in 1905.
At outside-right came George Badenoch, Chapman's former
colleague at Spurs, who could also play at half-back, and for
centre-half Chapman, in his first skilful capture, got the signature
of the Scot, David McCartney, 27, of Chelsea, beating several
other interested clubs. The left-half position was filled by fellow
Scot Fred McDiarmid, 26, another former Spurs colleague of
Chapman's well-known for his speed in track events: in 1905 he
took first prize in a 100-yard handicap for footballers.

It was not only in team-building that Chapman was taking a key
role. He was also developing a tactical plan that was to take the
Southern League by storm. Tactics were traditionally left to players
to work out, and as Chapman was still a player there was nothing
unusual in his involvement with this side of teamwork. But he was
also a manager, and a tactics-minded manager was unusual. The
starting point of his plan was a home defeat by Norwich in November 1907. It came at a time when injuries brought an end to Northampton's early run of success: Chapman himself was injured
during training but had to play because there was no one to take
his place.

The Canaries came onto the City Ground wearing their new
mustard-colour jerseys which had replaced blue and white stripes.
Yellow was adopted because it was more in keeping with Norwich's
nickname, a move ridiculed by *Punch* in a spoof report that, in
line with Norwich, Tottenham were to play with spurs on their
boots, Chelsea in pensioners' costumes and Southampton, the
Saints, in angel wings and haloes.

Northampton, however, did not find the Canaries amusing: the
defeat pushed them to fifth from bottom. The *Reporter* assured its
readers that 'brighter days will come along for the club Herbert
Chapman manages so well,' and its confidence was well-founded.
For the defeat confirmed Chapman's view that 'a team can attack

for too long'. Northampton's halves pressed forward too much behind the attackers, so Norwich were packed into their goal area. Chapman realized that a better plan was to drop back at times to open out the game and draw out the opposing defenders, and then to take swift advantage of the resulting gaps. And so out of defeat came a new, organic style of play, where forwards fell back to help the defence, as much to draw out the opposition as to block their advance. A year later, by Christmas 1908, the Town were Southern League leaders.

Chapman's first move in perfecting his combination after the Norwich defeat was to persuade his directors to pay £200 for Edward Lloyd Davies, Swindon's Welsh international full-back – who still holds the record as the club's most capped player. It was the first time Northampton had paid for a player. Transfer fees were not then the universal practice they were later to become, because players were tied to their clubs only for one season, after which they could join any other club they chose. And no transfer fees were paid when a player moved into the Southern League from the Football League.

But to get Lloyd Davies from Swindon in November 1907, Northampton had to pay a price. The £200 was an average sum (the first £1,000 transfer, when Middlesborough bought Alf Common from Sunderland in 1905, was still exceptional) but a serious strain on the finances of a small club like Northampton. To make up some of the money a club ladies' meeting planned for Easter 1908 a 'costume bazaar, entitled "By the shores of the Blue Mediterranean", with charming scenic effects'.

Cup training at Northampton was in keeping with the customary emphasis on general fitness, and included 'a spin round the County Ground track twice, followed by skipping and ball-punching, with a short walk into the country at the finish' (*Reporter*) and later a day in the country followed by a trip to Bedford for a Turkish bath. In December 1907 the Cobblers beat Sutton United 10–0 in the second round, still a record for the club, and were excused the qualifying rounds for the next season.

As he moved among the guests at goalkeeper Cooch's wedding in May 1908, Chapman must have realized that his own honey-

moon with Northampton Town was over. His first season as a
football manager had shown promise: now he needed to prove that
the Cobblers were no longer just another poor-to-average team but
a force to be reckoned with.

He had acquired new players, including a new inside-forward,
Lewis, from Coventry, beating Aston Villa and Bristol Rovers for
the twenty-one-year-old's signature. And this raised his hopes of
giving up playing himself to concentrate fully on management. His
early successes and his popularity with the players convinced the
Town directors of his worth, and they now viewed his appointment
as permanent. For his part, Chapman had become so involved
with the team in his charge that he gladly abandoned all thoughts
of the mining career he was about to embark on only a year before.
He became a father, too, in 1908, when his first son, Ken, was born.

The 1908–09 season saw the flowering of the new tactical plan
of sound defence and sudden, swift attacks built on long passing
and the element of surprise. Centre-half McCartney would move
forward to lure out the opposition then pass to Lewis on the right,
the opposing defenders following. Lewis would jab the ball to
McDiarmid, converted by Chapman from half-back to forward,
who would then drive it across goal. With the defence scattered, the
centre gave a scoring chance to at least three forwards.

The season was not without its curiosities. In a game at Norwich
the referee blew his whistle a full five minutes from time, and as
players and officials left the field Chapman approached him and
pointed out the error. The referee stuck to his decision but later,
when some players were already in the bath, he called both teams
back out onto the field to play another five minutes. Perhaps it was
this incident Chapman had in mind when he installed the big
clock at Highbury more than twenty years later.

For their Cup training, the Cobblers for the first time spent a
week away from Northampton. They decided against the abrupt
change of air of a seaside resort and went instead to Woburn Sands,
where the surroundings were quiet and the nearby pine forests provided a healthy atmosphere. They were eliminated from the competition by Derby County in a third round replay.

In the Southern League Championship, the club was more

successful. Despite further injuries, which forced Chapman to
continue playing, and a loss of form early in 1909, Northampton
were always in the race, their rivals being Swindon. The decisive
date was 20 April, when Northampton were away to Queen's
Park Rangers and Swindon away to Luton. Chapman's team won
their game but did not hear their rivals' result until they arrived
back at Northampton station to find hundreds of supporters
waiting to welcome them. Swindon had lost and Northampton
were champions.

It was a remarkable achievement. Only two years before, Northampton were in danger of relegation: now they were champions,
with a record 25 wins from 40 games, a record 55 points, and a
record 90 goals. The reserves also looked good for the future, winning the Northamptonshire League Championship. Lewis and
Lessons broke the club record for individual goal-scoring (beating
the 21 goals of Len Benbow in 1902–3), Lewis with 32, including
four hat-tricks, and Lessons with 24.

Chapman was not with his team to hear the cheers of the crowd
at the railway station. He was at Kiveton Park visiting his sick
father, and his pleasure at seeing Northampton top of the table
was tinged with sadness when his father died shortly after.

The Championship was won by a combination of efficient
teamwork and an honest belief in future success, both inspired and
developed by Chapman. He had learned the importance of teamwork in his playing days, and saw how individual talent could be
stifled by playing men in unsuitable positions, with complete disregard for their natural gifts. So he set out to create a single organic
unit in which each player was allotted his part according to his
particular talent. He had shown too his ability to choose, and get,
the right players for the team and, in the case of Lloyd Davies, to
back his judgement with hard cash, even if it meant stretching
club finances to the limit. But to avoid further cash buys, Chapman from the start encouraged local talent, organizing practice
matches before the start of the season to give trials to promising
youngsters from Northampton and the surrounding countryside.

Chapman played his last game as a professional on 23 January,
1909 (away to Watford), but he went on to play in amateur com-

petitions, even winning a few medals.

And he remained a devotee of clean play. Speaking to the footballers of Northampton Boys' Brigade, he told them: 'Never do
anything on the field to an opponent that will later prevent your
meeting him in the street or in church later and shaking hands
with him.' He expected the same impeccable conduct from his
own players. At the club reception on the night of the Championship win he spoke with pride about the behaviour of his men on
away visits. At every hotel they stayed at, he said, the proprietor
had been led to remark what 'a nice, quiet, gentlemanly lot of
fellows they were'.

Chapman also realized the importance of a happy family spirit
at the club, with directors, officials and players all pulling together for the common good. At Northampton there was not the
gulf that existed at other clubs between players and management,
and Chapman's psychological approach was appreciated by president Pat Darnell. At the Championship reception he spoke of the
manager's 'tact, judgement and discretion' and his 'consideration'
of the team. Earlier, when the team visited the Franco-British Exhibition at White City in September 1908 (Chapman wasn't
there: he had influenza) Darnell referred to the manager as the
players' 'friend at all times' and assured them they would be
'treated as men by the club whether they won or lost'.

In this, Chapman's own geniality served well, but he also put
the 'happy family' policy into general effect by arranging for improvements to the dressing-rooms and, under his trainer Dick Murrell, seeing that the players had quick, effective injury treatment.
In 1908 Chapman's brother Harry came to Northampton to make
use of the club's training facilities and to have his damaged knee
doctored. Prompt action was taken if an injury proved too serious
to be treated at the club, as when McDiarmid was taken to a
specialist in Sheffield in September 1907.

The public was also taken into consideration. Ground improvements were put in hand, new terracing built, and for a Cup tie
against Bristol Rovers in January 1908 carpets were laid in the
grandstand. When the Cup came round again the next year an
extra 300 seats were provided, bringing the total seating capacity

to 1,650. Chapman, aware of the value of publicity in stimulating interest in football, also made it his business to keep the local Press well informed of club news.

In both the running of the club and the style of football played on the field, most of the hallmarks of Chapman's style of management that were to become famous in later years were already appearing.

In 1909 Chapman had his first taste of European football. After a 2–0 defeat by League champions Newcastle in the Charity Shield at Stamford Bridge, the Northampton party left for a tour of Germany at the invitation of Nuremberg FC.

5

A MATCH FOR NEWCASTLE

Having scored his first major triumph in the Southern League Championship, Chapman began to question the merits of the framework of that triumph, that is, the Southern League itself. The competition lacked the prestige of the League Championship, and its future looked uncertain as one club after another abandoned it by successfully applying to enter the Football League – Bristol City in 1901, Chelsea in 1905, Fulham in 1907 and Tottenham in 1908. This influx of southern clubs ended the North's monopoly of the 'big' League, making it a more nationally representative competition, and eroding the standing of the Southern League.

In November 1911 Chapman added his own voice to many others suggesting plans for restructuring the entire league system. Some of these schemes involved a third division in the English League, but Chapman went further. He circulated clubs with a proposal that would set up, in effect, the system existing today, of four national divisions.

His plan was to reorganize the Southern League with other clubs into two divisions of eighteen to twenty clubs each, to be called the Football Alliance, with promotion and relegation between the Second Division of the League and the First of the Alliance as well as within the two organizations. In this way, thought Chapman, the Southern League, in its new guise, would provide greater competition within itself and would have greater command over its members' loyalty by providing automatic access for successful clubs to the League.

The plan enhanced Chapman's fame in the football world generally, but it was too radical to win immediate acceptance. The League clubs found the idea of relegation to what was in effect the

Southern League too terrible to contemplate. It was not until 1920 that a Third Division of twenty-two southern clubs was formed, with another of twenty-two northern clubs the following year. In 1950 the two Third Division sections were increased to twenty-four clubs each and in 1958 were replaced by the present Third and Fourth Divisions.

In later years Chapman came to realize that the extension of the league system was having a bad effect on the game. When he and others advocated extra divisions in the Edwardian period they could not have foreseen that the formation of a Third Division in 1920 would create an extra demand for players of talent at a time when a large part of the male population had been wiped out in a world war. This led to young players being drafted into top-class soccer before their abilities had had time to mature. Before 1920, writes Charlie Buchan in his autobiography, 'the county leagues had been the happy hunting grounds for the professional clubs. Scouts had only to go to the North-east, the Birmingham area or any of the thickly populated districts to discover several players almost up to the top League standard. But in the next few years, these areas were practically drained of their promising material. The standard of play dropped in the counties. There was keen competition among the big clubs to get any promising young player that came along.'[1]

Abolition of the Southern League also robbed players of a useful safety valve, for no transfer fee was payable when a player moved into it from the League. Under the old system, if a player was dissatisfied with his terms at a League club he could move to a Southern League team at the end of a season without waiting for a fee to be agreed.

Chapman came to criticize the league system most for making success the overriding consideration. Just as at Northampton he questioned the merit of the Southern League after shaping a team that mastered it, so after his later Championship triumphs at Huddersfield and Arsenal, he was to question the league system that was the framework of those triumphs.

He disliked the way clubs were compelled to concern themselves with points at the cost of skill, the restrictions imposed on development of young players by the prime importance of the first team, and the premature blooding of young players in the first team. He criticized in particular what he saw as the fundamental flaw in a system based on the pursuit of points: that a team was given a point before it even kicked a ball. It was an observation that has been sadly misinterpreted. His comment shows, say his critics, that Chapman's aim was to defend that point at all costs – he was thus a defensive-minded manager who set a bad example for football. He was not. Never at any time in his career did he set out solely to defend. His aim, from his Northampton days on, was a team that could switch quickly from attack to defence and back again as the game dictated: and the development of Arsenal's defence-in-depth system was matched by the creation of one of the most powerful forward lines in soccer history. He admired the traditional style of Scottish football for the 'finesse and cunning with which they invest their attack'. 'Their combined craftsmanship,' he said, 'makes for a spectacle that is all too rare on English fields.' [2]

But he saw that Scottish football too was on the decline and blamed the system of promotion and relegation introduced into the Scottish League in 1921. And he showed his cynical disregard for the system by suggesting that promotion and relegation should be on an eleven-up, eleven-down basis.

The enlargement of the Football League has had another effect that Chapman was to deplore – the escalation of transfer fees. This was bound to happen by the law of supply and demand, with too many League clubs chasing too few good players. In the pre-First World War days of two divisions, the top limit of transfer fees rose in the eight years from 1905 to 1913 from £1,000 to £2,500, an increase of 150 per cent; in the first eight years of three divisions (1920-28) they went up from £3,300 to £10,890, an increase of roughly 230 per cent. The rise has continued, reaching the £1½ million mark in 1980, accompanied by the customary, but vain, protests.

But as Chapman set about maintaining the momentum of his Northampton team after their 1909 Championship, and went in search of new players, transfer fees were not a problem. He made an exciting 'discovery' at Wellingborough. Outside-right Fred

'Fanny' Walden, 21, was just over five feet tall, weighed less than nine stone and looked easy meat for burly defenders. But what he lacked in build he made up for in speed and skill, nipping in and out of solid defences with astounding ease. He came into the North-ampton side at home to Luton on 30 October and scored a hat-trick in a 6–1 win, following this with another against Southend in December. And he cost Chapman next to nothing.

Walden was so small that on one occasion, entering the players' quarters behind his team-mates on arrival at an away game, he was told, 'Go away, sonny,' by an official. His size, combined with considerable talent, made him a popular figure at Northampton and Chapman called him a 'star artist' who could draw in the crowds and was 'largely the making of the Northampton team'. Walden, who also became a Northampton-shire County cricketer, went on to play for Tottenham. Billy Jones, a Spurs amateur centre-forward in the 1920s, remembers him for his clever ball control. 'He didn't score many goals but he was brilliant at laying on the ball for others. He was another Stanley Matthews.'[3] Walden was the first in a line of great Chapman dis-coveries.

Chapman also secured Barnsley goalkeeper Thomas Thorpe to replace Cooch, who went to Norwich.

The team continued to astound with their attacking flair and sound defence, treating the home crowd to wins of 5–1 over Ply-mouth, 10–1 over Croydon Common and 7–1 over New Bromp-ton. Their opponents, lacking the shrewd tactical direction and sense of purpose that Chapman provided, were slow to arm them-selves against the Cobblers' swift, sudden onslaughts. Most were still bewildered by the way Northampton opened out the game to create openings for surprise attacks, and after a 4–1 win at Swin-don, the Railwaymen's international winger Fleming told Chap-man: 'You have something more than a team: you have a machine.'

Despite these successes, Northampton's hopes of retaining the Championship faded as games were lost in March and April 1910. At Norwich, where they lost 2–0, the Cobblers played the first thirty minutes without their skipper McCartney – he had missed his train.

Northampton finished fourth, after finally ending the Norwich jinx with a 3–1 home win in the last game of the season, which brought a visit by 800 members of Norwich Supporters Club. To keep the supporters out of mischief during the morning, Chapman arranged tours of a local factory and brewery.

New players coming into the side in 1910 included half-back George Hampson, 21, from Oswestry, Frank Bradshaw, Sheffield Wednesday's international forward renowned for his fast solo runs, and right-back Fred Clipston, who cost £150 from Portsmouth. With Lloyd Davies in a new attacking role, the combination took time to settle, and crowds had to wait until the 1911–12 season to see the old magic at work again. Northampton finished third in 1912, with 82 goals, 41 against, maintaining the 2–1 average of the previous three seasons.

The league programme had not been free from the upsets that could arise from the organizational confusion of most Edwardian football clubs. On 1 October, 1910, Northampton were at home to Coventry City. Kick-off time was 3.30, but when the Cobblers took the field at 3.25, there was no sign of the Coventry party anywhere in the town.

Kick-off time passed, the crowd waiting patiently. Chapman recalled his players from the pitch. Over an hour later, the visitors finally arrived and both teams took the field – at two minutes to five. The City party had left Coventry on the two o'clock train, which was cheaper that the earlier ones but allowed no room for delay – and the engine broke down during the journey.

In the days before floodlighting it was obvious that a game starting at five o'clock could not possibly run its full course, but the referee went ahead, fearing trouble from a crowd that had waited over two hours. Inevitably, the game was finally abandoned because of bad light.

In an effort to retain the goodwill of supporters, Chapman wrote to the *Northampton Daily Echo*:

Sir – I am desired by the management of the Northampton Town Football Club to convey their sincere thanks to the supporters

present at the County Ground on Saturday last for the exemplary
patience shown awaiting the arrival of the Coventry team. The
cause of delay will be dealt with by the Southern League Management Committee in due course. I feel assured, however, no one
regrets the inconvenience and annoyance our supporters were
subjected to more than the Coventry executive. . . .

Yours, etc.

HERBERT CHAPMAN
(Secretary)

For the replay in December, Coventry travelled by express train
during the morning – and were beaten 4–1.

It was in the Cup that Northampton were now to make the
headlines. In 1910 they were drawn at home to First Division
Sheffield Wednesday. After losing centre-forward Lloyd Davies
with a knee injury, the Cobblers soldiered on with ten men to
earn a goalless draw. For the replay, Chapman made one of his
master-strokes, bringing McCartney out of the half-back line to
take Lloyd Davies's place at centre-forward. The result: a sen-
sational 1–0 victory. 'The match was won by absolutely unflinch-
ing work on the part of every player,' Chapman commented
proudly, as congratulatory telegrams flooded into his office.

Next hurdle was Nottingham Forest. Again the Cobblers held
them to a goalless draw after being reduced to ten men, but this
time it was not through injury: half-back Manning was sent off
after twenty-five minutes for tripping Forest's West from behind.
The *Daily Echo* protested that West was play-acting – he 'rolled
over and over as though in great bodily pain', then played a
'vigorous' game for the rest of the match. The paper reported that
the referee regretted his decision. And two FA officials were over-
heard to say that here was a case where, despite the laws forbid-
ding it, the ordered-off player should be allowed to come on again.
Northampton lost 1–0 in the replay – but the best was yet to come.

In the fourth round of the 1911 Cup competition, Northampton faced those giants of Edwardian football, Newcastle United,
away from home. Newcastle were the Cup holders, had been in
the final five times in seven years and were three times League

champions. They did sometimes falter against lesser teams, and in particular had a habit of losing to Crystal Palace in Cup ties, but Northampton were still rank outsiders, especially as their League performances were in the doldrums. The big day was February 4, and Chapman headed north with his team on the previous Thursday. On arrival at Newcastle station he told reporters: 'I hope my boys will give United a good game' – but beyond that he was 'courteously discreet and silent'. The visitors stayed at Tynemouth, where finishing touches were put to the plan of campaign, one of the main objectives being to beat the notorious Newcastle offside trap.

The 42,000 crowd saw two goals in as many minutes. Newcastle took the lead after a quarter of an hour, but a shot from Northampton's Bradshaw was too powerful for the keeper to hold and it went over his head into the net. There was an anxious moment for the Cobblers when Hampson had to be taken off, but he was soon back, and half-time arrived with the score still at 1–1. As the game wore on Northampton showed no signs of tiring. The razor-sharp accuracy of their passing pressurized and flummoxed Newcastle, reducing even the experienced full-back McCracken to kicking into touch. 'Tapper' of the *Northampton Daily Echo* wrote:

'This game was very much like a game of chess, with human beings as pieces. Though there was never-ceasing change, each movement was not a chance occurrence in a hotch-potch of bewildered uncertainty, but part and parcel of a pre-conceived plan, trimmed down or adorned to suit the particular circumstances of the moment. . . .

'I fancy it would have been a Palace final more worth watching than many a struggle at Sydenham. . . .

'The game presented a great contrast in styles. Newcastle were always striving to keep the ball by those machine-like movements which only the cleverest exponents of the short-passing game can exhibit. Northampton asked for no quarter and gave none. They stood on no ceremony. The defence infused a breathless energy into every move; they bustled the northern cracks into comparative impotence; they beat back this magnificent fighting line which has been the terror of a dozen clubs as a break-water hurls back the lashing waves.

'The forwards discarded seeking their end by devious ways. They wove no fancy patterns but, given the ball, straight they sped for goal. Just a brief run, enough to draw part of the defence towards the spot, and over it went with almost amazing accuracy to the other side of the field. There the operation was repeated. Backs of less experience than McCracken and Whitson would have been run off their legs long before this pair showed signs of flagging.'

Northampton came close to winning the game in the last five minutes when Walden drove a fierce shot against the crossbar, 'making a mark which it will take a paintbrush to efface'.

The draw was hailed as a 'magnificent achievement' by the *Echo*, which spoke of this 'historic day in the annals of the Northampton Town Club'. But the euphoria soon turned sour. In return for £900, Northampton, after consulting the players, waived ground rights for the replay and agreed to battle it out again at St James's Park. The sum was arrived at only after some haggling, Newcastle at first offering £400 and Northampton asking £1,000. It was not unusual to sell ground advantage, and the Town had special reason to accept the deal. Cup fever had obscured disappointing results and falling attendances in the League. At Christmas receipts were £500 below normal and the club owed £100 in rent to the County Cricket Club. On top of that, the first £100 instalment of a £600 interest-free loan for building the new stand was due to be repaid, and over £170 was owed to tradesmen. In all the club had debts totalling £4,000. The Town wanted to avoid selling players and could not lightly disregard the opportunity of securing bigger receipts from a capacity crowd at Newcastle. The club issued a statement explaining its move:

'Should we accept the offer or run the risk of being compelled to transfer players? Our policy has been to try to build up a great team and not to weaken our playing strength, and it was for this reason that we accepted the offer made. We believe on reflection that our supporters will recognize that our action has been actuated by the one desire to maintain first class soccer in Northants.'

But they could not avoid an outcry. Supporters attacked the decision as a short-sighted mistake, as the immediate monetary gain would be offset by low gates at home for the rest of the season. *The Athletic News* added its criticism, saying that Northampton Town had a duty to its supporters and that a visit by Newcastle to the County Ground would have helped to popularize football in Northampton.

The Cobblers again fought well in the replay, but lost by a disputed penalty. 'We were robbed out of the game,' said an angry Chapman.

Progress in the Cup the next year was more successful, if less spectacular. Northampton got to the fifth round for the first time after beating Bristol City (finalists in 1909) and then Darlington, in a replay at home. Before their first game against Darlington in February 1912, the Northampton squad stayed overnight at the seaside resort of Saltburn, in the grip of winter. They found the windows of their rooms frozen so hard they could not close them, and the players took their pre-match sleep with snow on the bedroom floor. The Cobblers finally went out of the competition at Fulham.

By then Chapman's name was being linked with Leeds City, and in May 1912 he accepted an offer to take over as secretary-manager of the Yorkshire club. His last move for Northampton was to beat several clubs to sign Nuneaton Town's inside-left Henry Smith.

Chapman's apprenticeship in football management was over. In five years he had turned a struggling side into formidable Championship contenders capable of springing surprises on League giants in the Cup. And the team's success created a new public for football in Northampton. Annual gate receipts rose during the period from £1,855 to £5,309, and 1912 saw the first four-figure profit – just over £1,000. This growth in revenue enabled a total of £2,500 to be spent on ground improvements.

It was the circumstances that made this achievement even more outstanding. First, the club could not afford large-scale spending on players: the payment of £200 for Lloyd Davies in 1907 strained its resources to the limit. In view of this, Chapman's

ability in getting maximum effort from the players available and
spotting talent in young players was vital. Second, Northampton
was predominantly a rugby centre. Town president Pat Darnell
was himself a rugby fan until he wandered into the soccer ground
at Leicester by mistake, and was converted. Most towns and
villages in the rest of the county had already turned to the association game by the turn of the century, but before 1907 their enthusiasm centred around their local teams. Only when the
Cobblers were doing well did county people go to Northampton,
hence the club's languishing state before Chapman took over.

The dichotomy between the rugby capital and the soccer county
was evident in February 1912 when Northampton had their replay with Darlington in the Cup. Several factories in Northamptonshire, anticipating the drift to the County Ground for the
mid-week game, closed down for the day, but in Northampton
itself factory workers were allowed the afternoon off only if they
made up for it in overtime. This pattern of support was a dangerous one for the club. If team performances slumped, as they did in
1910-11, attendances fell disastrously, sparking off a financial
crisis. It was as if Chapman were a captain trying to keep afloat
on a treacherous sea in a small boat that threatened at any moment
to spring a leak.

On Chapman's departure, the *Northampton Independent*
carried a tribute to him which recognized some of the essential
features of his managerial style:

'As a team manager, Mr Chapman has been strikingly successful, and he unites with his keen business abilities a winning
personality that makes him very popular. A fine judge of a player,
a skilled diplomatist, he has secured many good players for Northampton at very little cost to the club, whilst his tact and cheery
optimism has resulted in his getting the best out of the men at his
command.'

6

NEARLY PROMOTED

The news of Chapman's appointment was received in Leeds with eager anticipation. The secretary-managership of Leeds City had become vacant on the retirement of Scott Walford at the end of the club's most disastrous season since it entered the Second Division eight years before, and the public looked with keen interest to see what effect the new man's 'shrewd judgement and tactful management' (*Yorkshire Post*) would have. 'Leeds City can congratulate themselves on securing such a man as Mr Chapman,' commented *The Athletic News*.

From Chapman's point of view, the appointment offered a higher salary, a move to his native Yorkshire and an alluring challenge similar to that he faced at Northampton in 1907, with the added prestige of League status. His aim was clear: 'I am here to get Leeds City into the First Division. It is, of course, a matter of time, but if it is humanly possible, it shall be attained.'

It was an ambitious aim, for Leeds were in the ignominious position of seeking re-election, and Chapman spent the rest of May canvassing for votes. Leeds were re-elected, with thirty-three votes, along with Lincoln City, at a Football League meeting on 4 June (which also heard that the League had raised £696 for the victims of the *Titanic* disaster).

Chapman took over at Leeds at a time when professional footballers were beginning to assert themselves as an organized body of workers. A players' union (the present Professional Footballers' Association) was formed in 1907, after an earlier, unsuccessful attempt in 1898. The union was recognized by the FA, but when it affiliated to the Federation of Trade Unions, recognition was withdrawn and players were told to resign from the union or be banned from football. At a time of militant unionism in the country generally, both the FA and the Football League feared disruption of the football programme if the players' union got involved with disputes in other industries. The result was a threatened players' strike in 1909, which led the authorities to re-recognize the union.

It was in this period too that a club's control over a player was first challenged in the law courts. In the case of Lawrence Kingaby *v.* Aston Villa in 1912, the player claimed damages for loss of employment, because the club had put 'too high' a transfer fee on him which prevented him taking an offer from another club. Judgement was in favour of Aston Villa and it was not until fifty years later that a fresh legal challenge over contract terms was made, by George Eastham against Newcastle United.

Leeds City, or the Peacocks as they were known from the gold V-shaped band on their blue strip, climbed to a more secure position in mid-table in the months after Chapman took over. But the side was as yet inconsistent, the combination unbalanced. Of the attack the *Yorkshire Post* commented: 'The present players will never blend, as their styles are so dissimilar. Individualism is by no means to be deprecated, but cohesiveness should be the first aim of an attacking line.' Disappointed supporters demanded to know why Chapman had not signed any new players since the summer. It was not, he answered, through want of trying: clubs were either unwilling to sell so early in the season, or were asking too high a fee. Even junior clubs were holding on to their players. It would not, he admitted, be hard to find players who were 'fairly good', but they would not strengthen the team: nothing but the best would do. Then in November came a golden opportunity.

Northampton Town, languishing since Chapman's departure and losing money at the rate of £30 a week, were open to offers for Fanny Walden. Chapman jumped at the chance, but the Cobblers' supporters were determined that Walden should stay, and a 'shilling fund' was set up to thwart the designs of their former manager. It worked, and by the end of the month the deal was off.

'In no instance have I personally suffered so great a disappointment,' Chapman confessed. But he remained hopeful of securing

Walden in the future, for he 'would be the making of the Leeds City team if only I could get him to Elland Road'. The player did eventually join the Peacocks, but under unusual and unforeseen circumstances.

Chapman aimed to finish the season among the top five so that his players would qualify for bonuses under a new League scheme. Promotion, he predicted, would come within two seasons. In pursuit of this, he renewed his efforts to get new players, and was rewarded with two promising youngsters, outside-right Bainbridge, from Seaton Delaval, and inside-right Price, from Worksop. But his first star signing for Leeds was James Speirs, at twenty-six Bradford City's top scorer and one of the best inside-lefts in the country. Formerly of Glasgow Rangers, he captained the Cup-winning Bradford City side of 1911, but an 'incompatability of temper' led to his transfer for £1,400. Chapman had kept a close watch on Speirs' feud with Bradford City, and moved in just at the right moment. 'The enterprise of the Leeds City management in securing Speirs would have staggered those responsible for the club a few years ago,' observed the *Yorkshire Evening Post*.

Another forward signed by the new manager was George Fenwick, 20, an outside-left who, since the start of the season, had scored 17 goals for Shildon, County Durham.

Chapman, said the *Yorkshire Post*, was 'slowly but surely evolving a set of players from whom much may be expected in the future'.

He had, however, concentrated entirely on improving his forward line, neglecting a shaky defence. The result was the extraordinary situation at the end of March 1913, when goals for equalled goals against at 56. Leeds finished sixth, one place below Chapman's target. Goals totalling 70 broke the club record, but goals conceded were also up, at 63. Top scorer, with 26, was McCleod, whose play improved considerably with the introduction of new players, especially Speirs. McCleod was widely regarded as one of the best centre-forwards in the country, and several clubs were interested in him. Since coming to Leeds from Lincoln City for £500 in 1906, McCleod had scored 117 League goals in more than 200 games by the time a benefit match was held for him in April 1913. The game, against Nottingham Forest, was arranged the previous October when the player was guaranteed £350, although the target was set at £500. McCleod scored the only goal, and takings were over £750.

'Much praise' was owed to Chapman for Leeds' improved performance, said the *Yorkshire Evening News*. He was the 'guiding light' who 'has done a tremendous amount of good work for the club; he has gained the confidence of everyone'. Not least, he had gained the confidence of the directors, for his outlay of £3,000 for new players was offset by gate receipts almost double those of the previous season, producing £400 profit, the best since 1907.

Chapman acknowledged the 'splendid support' that had rallied to the club, but he regarded the Elland Road spectators, in common with other Yorkshire crowds, as too partisan. He wished they would show more appreciation of the skills of visiting teams and more tolerance of mistakes by their own players. 'To howl down a man just because he happens to be out of form one day is often sufficient to discourage him for all time,' he told the *Yorkshire Evening Post*. Barracking, one of Chapman's pet hates, was particularly active at reserve matches, and he declared that a close watch would be made for offenders.

The promises of Chapman's first season at Leeds were marred by a major blackspot, a shadowy portent of the catastrophe to come. On 9 October, 1912 the Football League appointed a commission to inquire into alleged illegal payments by the club. When Chapman had signed on new players in July, he had agreed to pay three of them the full yearly wage of £208 to the end of the next April. But as two months had already elapsed since the end of the previous contracts, this would mean that for some weeks the players would be getting more than the permitted £4 a week maximum. Aston Villa were fined for making similar payments, and Chapman realized the illegality of his own action. He got the board to take the initiative in asking for a League inquiry, hoping that in return the sentence would be a light one.

The result was an unexpectedly heavy fine of £125 plus the expenses of the commission. Chapman and two of the players were censured and all three players ordered to refund their excess wages – which in effect saved the club over £100 towards the fine. The commission, 'while finding it necessary to admonish Mr Chapman and two of the players . . . also recognized the straightforwardness of Mr Chapman in reporting the matter. He adopted an honourable course, which is greatly to his credit and that of the club.'

The sentence could have been much worse. In 1904, shortly after winning the FA Cup, Manchester City lost its entire team as punishment for illegal bonus payments to players. The secretary and some directors were suspended and most of the players, including the great Billy Meredith, went to arch-rivals Manchester United. For Leeds City, however, the worst was yet to come.

An aftermath of the season was the award of another benefit match, for the outside-left Croot, who had been with the club seven years. It was held the following April against Arsenal and gave Croot £250. The benefit match was an essential ingredient both in Chapman's policy of raising the club's image in the estimation of the players and in his policy of attracting top-class talent to Elland Road. 'It is important if Leeds City is to be made attractive to good footballers that the club should have the reputation of conferring good benefits,' he told the *Yorkshire Evening Post*.

Chapman insisted that he was interested only in the best players, and he was prepared to go anywhere to get them. At first, he was sympathetic to the 'popular cry that the premier team has not tried to encourage and develop local talent', and assured readers of the club programme that steps were being taken to foster such talent. He suggested to the Leeds and District Football Association that they should field a representative side against Leeds City reserves, a game duly held at Elland Road, but he soon became disillusioned. Fostering local talent, he said later, was 'all very well in theory, but in practice it will not pay', because the talent to make Leeds City a successful team did not exist locally. 'I am rather inclined to think that the working conditions in this part of the country are opposed to the development of first class footballers,' he said. Factories in the West Riding kept young employees at work until the early evening, leaving little time and energy for soccer practice.

Another reason for the dearth of soccer talent in Leeds was the predominance of rugby. In September 1912 the Leeds and District FA expressed concern at the takeover of practice pitches by Rugby Union clubs, and urged senior soccer clubs to provide grounds for junior players.

Nevertheless, Chapman remained convinced that Leeds would become 'as great a centre of Association Football as any city in England'. It was a prediction that was to take half a century to be fulfilled – with Leeds United.

As Saturday in the Leeds of 1913 was a day of football – association or rugby – so Sunday was a day of religious devotion. Chapman, along with many footballers, went to church regularly, but half-back and captain Lintott made a more positive contribution to Sunday worship – as a popular preacher. 'A man of culture – he is a teacher in one of Bradford's schools – he has a ready command of language,' and by his work, said the *Yorkshire Evening Post,* had raised the status of the professional player. The idea of a preaching footballer strikes an odd note in more modern times, when players, though more educated and considerably richer than their forebears, engage in outside interests of a more commercial nature. Arthur Bridgett, from Sunderland, another newcomer to Leeds City, was also a preacher. Such activities, not uncommon among players, were the working-class answer to the 'muscular Christianity' of the nineteenth-century public schools and helped to make soccer more socially acceptable among the 'respectable' classes.

In the summer of 1913 Chapman at last turned his attention to City's unsound defence. Full-back Albert Unwin, 19, signed professional forms for Leeds, rejecting the attentions of Sheffield United, Middlesborough, Bristol City and Tottenham – all First Division clubs. Unwin had played in the South Bank team that had won the West Riding Junior Cup in 1912 and the Amateur Cup the next year.

In August Chapman signed his former half-back George Hampson from Northampton, and although his previous visit to Northampton had failed to secure Walden – he went to Tottenham in April for £1,750 – the developing form of Bainbridge at outside-right more than made up for the disappointment. Other newcomers were amateur winger Ivan Sharpe from Derby County, who worked in a newspaper office, and centre-half Harry Peart, 23, from neighbours Bradford City, who excelled at turning defence quickly into attack with a well-placed header. The team promised much as Leeds made another bid for promotion.

In this endeavour Chapman was to meet some brotherly rivalry. Harry Chapman had taken over as secretary of Hull City alongside team manager Ambrose Langley, after injury ended three years as a Hull player. In October Hull knocked Leeds out of the West Riding Cup and – with an under-strength side – inflicted the Peacocks' first home defeat of the season. But Leeds looked set fair for the First Division, climbing to second place by the end of the year. Chapman brought in more new players to maintain the challenge. Inside-right John Jackson, 23, came from Clyde for £1,000, one of Leeds' largest outlays, and Fred Blackman, described by the *Yorkshire Post* as 'possibly the most stylish and polished back in the Second Division', was bought from Huddersfield Town. The fee for Blackman was said to be over £1,000, and only £300 less than the existing Leeds record. In the end the Peacocks finished fourth; Chapman's promotion bid had, only narrowly, failed.

It was during this season that Chapman made his first visit to Highbury, the new home of the newly-relegated Arsenal. When Leeds City arrived for their meeting with the Gunners (which they lost 1–0), on 6 December, 1913, the Highbury ground was still only half-finished and a wooden stand on the east side, designed for 9,000 spectators, was still being built. Chapman was particularly struck by the fact that the ground was just across the road from Gillespie Road Underground station, and could thus be reached easily from most parts of London. This observation was to bear fruit in later years.

At home Leeds were in more trouble with the authorities, this time over a dispute with Fulham. Leeds couldn't immediately pay Fulham their share of the takings for the match at Elland Road on Christmas Day, so Fulham retaliated by withholding

money from Leeds after the return match at Craven Cottage on
Boxing Day. At an FA inquiry in February, City pleaded that,
because of a tram strike on Christmas Day, the crowd arrived
late for the match and there were no police to stop them rushing
the ground. Some admission money had to be taken 'on account',
so the club couldn't pay Fulham their due straight away. Fulham
were ordered to pay the overdue sum, amounting to £20 4s 5d,
plus three guineas expenses, and Leeds were reprimanded for not
taking money at the gates.

Chapman laid part of the blame for not winning promotion on
the loss of two vital points at Clapton Orient in March, at a
crucial stage in the race. As the game was on a Monday, Orient
insisted on a kick-off at 4.30, to stand a better chance of a good
gate. After some argument they agreed to 4.20, but the referee and
linesman arrived five minutes late. The game was further delayed
when the referee ordered Leeds goalkeeper Scott to change his
jersey, in keeping with the League rule of 1909 that keepers must
wear distinctive colours. By the time Scott had changed his blue
jersey for something less like the blue and gold of his colleagues,
the ten minutes' grace had been swallowed up. By half-time it
was obvious the rest of the game would continue in darkness, and
to save time the referee ordered the players to stay on the field
for an interval of two minutes only. 'By a quarter to six,' the *Yorkshire Post* reported, 'it was practically impossible to distinguish
players in midfield' and the teams were like 'moving figures in
shadowland'.

As the gloom thickened, Leeds, a goal up, suddenly conceded
three in quick succession, and the game ended in victory for
Orient. The result stood because the referee, after consulting his
linesmen, decided that Scott could have seen the ball coming at
him. A furious Chapman regarded the affair as an outrage, and
assured the referee he would lodge an appeal against 'this insult'.
The appeal, considered a fortnight later, was upheld and Clapton
Orient were fined £25. The incident goes a long way to explaining Chapman's later enthusiasm for floodlit football.

Ultimately, however, the underlying reason for the narrow
failure to win promotion in 1914 was the inadequate reserve

strength at City's disposal: the reserves finished bottom in their
competition. A step in remedying the situation was taken in
March when John Chaplin, a former Spurs, Manchester City and
Dundee player, was appointed assistant trainer with special responsibility for the reserves.

Despite the Peacocks' less than perfect performances Chapman's achievement in two years was no less remarkable than that
at Northampton in the same space of time. He may not have won
a championship, but he had taken Leeds from bottom of the table
to fourth, their highest position ever, in a much stiffer competition
than the Southern League. Financial limitations and unwilling-
ness to sell made new players increasingly hard to find, in an area
where, as Chapman pointed out, industrial conditions were not
conducive to home-grown talent, and where there was strong
competition from rugby.

Yet against all these odds bigger crowds were coming to Elland
Road, and the ground was smartened up to give it the image of a
major sports centre. A new flag was bought for the masthead and a
scheme put in hand to cover part of the terraces. The prestige of
Elland Road was further enhanced when the Amateur Cup final
was staged there in 1914.

More important, there were innovations behind the scenes,
marking a new development in Chapman's style of management.
It was at Leeds that he came to realize the value of a game of golf
in relaxing his players, and in 1913 he introduced a day's golf each
week as part of regular training. Another, more startling, departure was the introduction of regular team talks, the idea for which
came on a train travelling back from an away match. Observing a
heated argument among the players over a game of cards, Chapman thought that if they put as much consideration and earnestness into their football, their game could only improve. Meetings
were accordingly held each week to discuss both the previous game
and the tactics to be used in the next. With Chapman presiding,
every player was encouraged to express his own opinion. This was
something entirely new in football, a marked contrast to the prevailing easy-going system where players were left to work out their
own tactics. In holding the talks Chapman was asking his players

to contribute to a joint effort, to become more involved with each other as a unit. It was an appeal to intelligence as well as physical skill, and it had the effect of boosting self-respect, fostering a sense of loyalty, and raising a player's status above that of a mere paid servant.

7

IN WARTIME

The summer of 1914 started very much like any other, with Chapman passing the long sunny days playing cricket and golf with his players and keeping them in trim for the coming season. But unknown to him the fate of Leeds City was no longer in his hands; it was being decided, along with that of every other club in the country, by a totally unrelated event in a faraway city in Eastern Europe. The assassination of the heir to the Austrian throne in Sarajevo on 28 June set the European powers at each other's throats, and in little over a month Great Britain was at war with Germany. Words familiar to the football follower, like 'victory', 'campaign' and 'tactics', now had very different connotations.

Britain was the only country entering the war without compulsory military service. As the football season approached, the question arose whether the League competition should be suspended so that players and officials could be free to volunteer for the war effort. It was a situation organized football had never had to face before, and there was no precedent on which to base a decision. Flying in the face of public opinion and patriotic fervour, the authorities decided to go ahead with games as planned.

The reaction was one of violent denunciation. Newspapers said they would not report matches and carried a barrage of irate letters. A *Yorkshire Post* reader suggested that the King should resign as patron of the Football Association. At the same time the FA urged 'players and spectators who are physically fit and otherwise able to join the Army', and several players did so, but the Football League insisted that 'in the interests of the people of this country football ought to be continued'.

The League's attitude reflected the traditional belief that the ordinary citizen need not be affected by war. Wars had been fought before by the regular Army, and this one, it was supposed, would be the same: it would be over in a few months, it not weeks. So League teams kicked off in the usual way, while the guns blazed across the Channel. After a few weeks newspapers lifted their ban on match reports, and while the war was waged on the front page, the struggle for League points gathered pace on the back.

Chapman, his players and fellow officials joined the civilian army and donated five per cent of their wages to the national relief fund, while Elland Road was used for military drill and firing practice.

In these circumstances it was hard to concentrate on football, and the standard of play fell. Players were depressed by lingering public indignation at playing the sport in wartime, and gates slumped by as much as 50 per cent.

As a result, the Football League proposed a cut in wages and in October Coventry City players became the first to accept a reduction. The League drew up a scale of reductions whereby players on £5 a week (the maximum) took a 15 per cent cut and those on £3–4 a 5 per cent cut, the money saved going into a fund to help clubs in financial straits. The scheme was criticized by Second Division Clubs on the grounds that they had to share the onus equally with the better-off. Leeds City players refused to accept the cuts, saying that such action should be voluntary.

Despite losing Lintott to the Forces, new Leeds players gave the *Yorkshire Post* confidence 'that in the near future the various parts necessary to make a harmonious whole will be welded together'. And before long Leeds were in the final of the West Riding Cup, their opponents being Hull City. (Harry Chapman was no longer with the club, ill health forcing him to an early retirement.) Leeds won the game, in pouring rain, before a crowd of a mere 1,000, by a single goal scored by Speirs.

The aftermath of the cup win was not without incident. As the players left the field after a game at Bury, Speirs and a Bury player got into a violent argument, and when the Leeds players reached their dressing-room they found their way blocked by a hostile crowd of home supporters. A serious incident was averted,

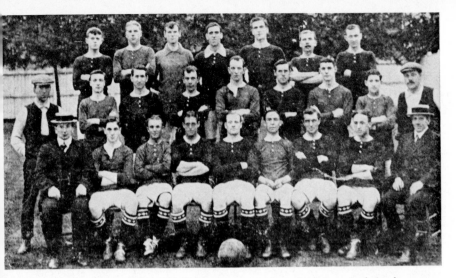

4 Northampton Town, 1910-1911. Chapman is seated at the left end of the front row. Standing behind him is Dick Murrell, the trainer. Fred Walden (third from left, front row) and Lloyd Davies (second from right, back row) are also in the photograph.

5 Huddersfield Town, 1921-1922. *Left to right, back row*: D. Parker, R. Mitchell, W. Dawson, J. Barlow, A. B. Hirst, J. H. Raynor, H. Robinson; *middle row*: J. W. Wood, C. Slade, A. Mutch, T. Wilson, W. Watson, S. J. Wadsworth; *front row*: Herbert Chapman, G. E. Richardson, F. D. Mann, E. Islip, C. Stephenson, W. H. Smith, J. E. Chaplin (trainer).

6 Herbert Chapman (seated, front left) and the Huddersfield Town players at Skelmanthorpe in 1925.

7, 8 Herbert Chapman in 1925. The cartoon accompanied the *Huddersfield Daily Examiner's* announcement of his move to Arsenal.

however – although one 'threatening individual' was detained –
and officials managed to clear a way through. Both Leeds and
Bury were angry at some of the referee's decisions in the game,
and reported him to the League for 'indifferent refereeing'.

Much more serious was the turn the war had taken. As the rival
armies became entrenched in the battlefields of France, the realization dawned that hostilities would last a lot longer than at first
thought. Lord Kitchener, who warned that the war would last
three years and not three months, launched a recruitment campaign in September 1914 which by the end of November had
created an army of some 100,000 volunteers. The commanding
Kitchener forefinger emerging from street hoardings put psychological pressure on all to enlist, including football spectators and
players, and pointed to the eventual closure of League soccer.

Leeds' outstanding win of the season was a 6–2 victory at Hull,
their first win there, their biggest ever away score and Hull's
heaviest home defeat. McCleod broke the club's individual record
by scoring five of the six goals. But the triumph was watched by
only 5,000, half of whom were soldiers in uniform.

At the end of March 1915 the FA decreed that no wages were
to be paid to players during May, June and July, and reduced the
maximum wage further from £4 to £3. An embargo was put on
transfers until August. At the same time the Football League introduced a plan for the maximum weekly wage to increase by ten
shillings every two years, with an ultimate ceiling of £260 a year.

March also saw developments for Leeds City reserves, when
the club resigned from the Midland League to switch to the more
suitable Central League. Application was made two months later,
and, in accordance with the rules, Chapman resigned from the
Central League management committee.

Leeds finished a poor fifteenth in the Second Division in 1915.
Wartime conditions had robbed players of the incentive to win
promotion because of the uncertain future of League football, and
caused a sharp fall in gates which made it virtually impossible to
spend money on improving the team. Set against wage reductions
and the receipt of several hundred pounds from the League relief
fund was an average gate yield of less than £200. But other clubs

facing similar conditions had done better than Leeds. And the
factory hours and rugby support which militated against soccer in
Leeds had been challenged with some success from 1912 to 1914.

A more likely explanation for the slump can be found in the
shaky financial structure of the club, which made it hard for
Chapman to act with any confidence. For some time financial
control had been in the hands of a receiver after the Leeds City
company was wound up. In August 1915 the receiver, Mr
Coombes, decided he could no longer continue in charge of the
club and offered to sell it to the Leeds Northern [Rugby] Union
Club at Headingley, who were interested.

But Leeds City found a saviour in Mr J. Connor, secretary of the
West Riding Football Association, who with four other local
citizens decided to form a syndicate, with himself as chairman, to
keep the club at Elland Road, and to set up a limited liability
company. Connor was seen as a 'valuable acquisition' and the
'responsible and qualified adviser from a football standpoint
which Mr Herbert Chapman has needed'. As *The Athletic News*
pointed out, City's future now seemed more assured, with the
growing popularity of soccer in Leeds and a 'progressive manager'
in Chapman.

That summer football waited anxiously for a decision on the
future of the League competition. Some players had taken jobs in
arms factories, others had enlisted (as early as October 1914 some
70,000 players had already joined the Forces). The authorities
had no option but to suspend the League, replacing it with three
regional leagues in which men could play as amateurs, receiving
only a token payment plus expenses, wherever they happened to
be stationed. There were to be no Cup ties.

Leeds City, whose wartime league was to be the Midland
Section, were not very hard hit by the dispersal of players. Some,
including McCleod, were working at local engineering firms, and
Wainwright at a nearby khaki factory. Price was working in
Sheffield but was willing to help out from time to time. But Speirs,
the captain, was lost when he enlisted in Glasgow with the
Cameron Highlanders.

Following Speirs's departure, Fanny Walden offered his services to City while working with a nearby firm of motor engineers. Tottenham were furious and protested to the League, only to be told that under wartime regulations it was perfectly in order. Not to be put off, Spurs urged the FA to hold an inquiry – but to no avail. Walden made his Leeds City debut in September 1915 at Derby, in a 3–1 win. Chapman had at last got the player he had wanted for so long.

Leeds had a good start in the new competition, climbing to second place after a 7–1 win over Barnsley in October, in which Price got five of the goals.

In wartime conditions the fostering of local talent, which Chapman had abandoned as a main source of players in peacetime, became a necessity, and local football was boosted when Chapman arranged for City reserves to meet elevens from West Riding organizations. By October local players were establishing themselves in the City reserves.

These reserve games were not without incident. In a match at Elland Road Wainwright was given his marching orders for swearing after an offside decision – but refused to go. The mortified referee ordered the game to end but then was persuaded to leave while one of the linesmen took over, a spectator taking the linesman's place. Wainwright had nothing to lose by his insubordination as it was his last game for Leeds: he had enlisted with the Royal Garrison Artillery and left for Dover two days later.

Chapman lost another key player when McCleod, though still working in Leeds, decided to play for City's neighbours and rivals Bradford (Park Avenue). His action was popularly resented as a poor show of gratitude for the benefit he had been given two years before.

Meanwhile the politics of war had taken a new departure. Although Kitchener's recruitment campaign was bringing in more men than the Army could properly train and equip (by January 1916 two and a half million men had enlisted), public pressure was mounting for conscription. In a last attempt to avoid this very un-English measure the Liberal Government introduced a scheme, organized by Lord Derby, whereby men 'attested' their willingness to serve if called upon. In December 1915 Chapman, Connor and

most of the City players 'attested'. Conscription was finally
brought in the following March.

The rest of the season saw more coming and going among
players, with the balance tilted against City. The international
winger Sergeant George Wall of the 11th Black Watch and
Manchester United offered to play for City but the taxi sent to
collect him from the station waited in vain. The soldier wrote to
Chapman that, because of military duties, he couldn't play after
all. In February Chapman got a promise of help from Clem
Stephenson, the Aston Villa inside-forward from Seaton Delaval,
Northumberland, who was to play such a crucial part in the rise
of Huddersfield Town. In one game, against Nottingham
Forest, Stephenson was joined by another player who was to take
a leading role in Chapman's future – Grenadier Guardsman
Charlie Buchan of Sunderland, whom Chapman met for the first
time.

In March 1916 the Midland League programme was completed, and to fill the remaining weeks of what used to be the
normal season a subsidiary tournament involving six clubs was
organized, with Leeds City in the Northern Group of the Midland
League. Leeds did well, but it looked as though top points would
be shared with Huddersfield as, on the last Saturday of the tournament, the Peacocks were away to Bradford City while Huddersfield, two points behind, were home to Bradford (Park Avenue).
But Huddersfield lost and Leeds won, to take the subsidiary league
championship outright, with 15 points from 10 games. It was to
be the last triumph Chapman was to see at Elland Road, for in the
summer of 1916 he took a managerial job at a munitions factory
at Barnbow, near Leeds. At the same time Walden joined the air
section of the Royal Naval Reserves.

With his practical knowledge of mining engineering and his nine
years as a football manager, Chapman was well equipped to deal
with the demands of industrial management. The Barnbow factory
made shells, and Chapman became virtually its manager-in-chief,
with some thirty sub-managers under him. And just as in football
he knew how to get the most out of his resources, so in the factory
he used his skills to obtain maximum production. By the end of the

war the factory had produced more shells than any other of its size, and at 25 per cent less cost, while the output of ammunition boxes had more than quadrupled.

On leaving Leeds City, Chapman recommended as his deputy George Cripps, a schoolteacher and one of his assistants. He continued to advise the club from Barnbow. At the end of the first month of the 1916-17 season City reached new goal-scoring heights, showing a 'superiority over the opposition to an extent seldom met with in first class football' (*Yorkshire Evening News*).

For Chapman the successes were marred by the death of his brother Harry, from tuberculosis, at the age of thirty-six. A short time before his death Harry Chapman had left his Hampshire rest home to stay at Herbert's home in Oakwood, Leeds, and the care with which he was attended in his last days showed his elder brother's family loyalty and devotion. Next-door neighbour Miss Gwendoline Wilkinson recalls: 'It was wonderful the way Herbert Chapman looked after his brother. I shall always think of him with admiration.' Harry Chapman's wife had died the previous year, and the couple left three children.

Leeds City went on to clinch the Midland League championship in 1917 and next season won the 'double' of both Midland League and subsidiary tournaments. They were also declared League champions in a new competition in which winners of the Midland and Lancashire sections played each other on a home-away basis.

City beat Stoke 2–1 on aggregate. Sad to say, these successes were to be the prelude to the downfall of Leeds City.

8

DISGRACE

The storm clouds gathering over Leeds City broke almost a year after the end of the First World War. In October 1919 an inquiry began into allegations that City had broken wartime regulations by paying players more than the permitted rates. A joint commission of the FA and Football League ordered the accounts for the years 1916 to 1918 to be produced in evidence, and when these were not forthcoming expelled the club from the League. Chapman and Cripps, together with Connor and three other members of the syndicate, were banned from attending football matches and taking part in football management. It looked as though Chapman's soccer career was at an end.

At the time of the inquiry Chapman was no longer manager of Leeds City. In the summer of 1918 he began to devote more time to the club in between duties at the arms factory in Barnbow, but, perhaps sensing that trouble was brewing, he suddenly resigned as secretary-manager on 16 December to go into full-time industrial management with Joseph Watson & Sons at the Olympia oil and cake works in Selby. The possibility of returning to football later was then still open. The *Yorkshire Evening News* spoke of him as the man whose motto was 'keep smiling'. 'No player, at a moment that mattered, ever saw Herbert Chapman with a long face. Outwardly, at least, he was an optimist in the darkest moments.'

A week after Chapman's resignation George Cripps also left the club, after handing over the books for the previous two years to Mr J. W. Bromley, a former director. Connor said later that Cripps pointed out unlawful payments recorded in the books to Bromley but promised not to mention them outside the club. Bromley claimed that he then handed the books over to Alderman (later

Sir William) Clarke, a solicitor, on condition they were not to be
shown to anyone without the consent of himself and the syndicate.
In return the syndicate donated £50 to the Leeds General
Infirmary. In July 1919, the Leeds City full-back Charles Cope-
land, dissatisfied with his contract, reported the club to the
authorities.

Bromley said he was willing for the documents to be shown to
the inquiry, but the syndicate could not agree. The commission
had no choice but to expel City from the League for, as League
President John McKenna explained, to have allowed the club to
continue would have set a precedent for other clubs to withhold
their books. McKenna told the *Yorkshire Post*:

'Leeds City could not be suspended as a club – we had no
power to do that; but so long as they refused to give up those vital
papers, we could have no way out save by expelling them.

'The authorities of the game intend to keep it absolutely clean.
We will have no nonsense. The football stable must be cleansed
and further breakages of the law regarding payments will be dealt
with in such a severe manner that I now give warning that clubs
and players must not expect the slightest leniency. . . .

'Every member of the commission was sorry that Leeds had to
be dealt with at all. We recognized that they had gone through
troublous times before.

'We recognized that they were a new club, that they had
obtained a good holding in a Rugby area and that the club had
bright prospects, but our case was clear – Leeds were defiant, and
could be defiant through one cause – fear of the papers giving
away certain secrets.'

Leeds City's fixtures were taken over by Port Vale, while the
players were auctioned at the Hotel Metropole in the strangest
football sale of the century. Leeds, bereft of professional soccer
despite the Lord Mayor's gallant attempt to keep City a going
concern outside the League, became the focus of attention of
managers everywhere. Within a week of the inquiry Chapman's
former stars were snapped up at bargain prices totalling £10,150,
the highest fee, £1,250, being paid by Notts County for McCleod.
Bainbridge went to Preston and Price to Sheffield Wednesday for

£1,000 each, while Hampson joined Aston Villa for £800. It was the final ignominy in the short, troubled history of the club that nearly made it to the First Division.

Of the six men banned, Chapman was probably least involved, as he was away from the club when the malpractices allegedly took place. Connor put the blame for the 'hopeless' state of the books on Cripps who, on Chapman's return in 1918, was allowed to remain an assistant but, because of his alleged mismanagement, was forbidden to travel with the team. According to Connor, Hampson threatened a players' strike unless the travel ban was lifted but after a rebuke from Chapman acquiesced in the situation.

Cripps denied that the books had been improperly kept, saying that an accounts clerk had been appointed to look after them after his own health had broken down in 1917. Chapman came back the next year, he said, because he had more time, not because the finances were in a muddle. Cripps's loss to soccer was rugby's gain; he spent the next twenty years teaching that branch of football to schoolboys.

The truth about the wartime payments remained hidden with the documents, and the extent of Leeds City's guilt (if any) has never been discovered. In any case, it must have been a question of degree. Wartime rules stated that only token payment plus expenses were to be paid, but clubs, like any other employers, can choose to be as generous or mean with expenses as with wages. It was widely believed that City were no more guilty than a great many other clubs keen to do well in the emergency competitions. If this were so then these other clubs must have breathed a sigh of relief when City's books were not produced. They elected Leeds United, formed shortly after the demise of City, to the Second Division in 1920, less than a year later, a move popularly interpreted among supporters as gratitude. George Cripps's son wrote to the *Yorkshire Post* in October 1979: 'The remarks of Mr J. McKenna make me smile when I remember some of the things which my father told me about the machinations by various members of the then Football League, which have certainly led me to believe that they were not so simon pure as the image they presented to the public.'

Chapman continued with his industrial work, but he had to

carry the stigma of the commission's verdict. It must have been distasteful for a man whose principles were always of the very highest. He was soon to clear his name, however, with momentous consequences for the soccer world from which he had been expelled.

9

THE FIRST CUP

His football career in ruins, Chapman stood at the threshold of a new decade in a cloud of uncertainty. His job at Selby, though it had none of the glamour of his former work, at least enabled him to provide for his family of two sons, Ken and Bruce, and daughters Mollie and Joyce. Late in 1920, however, the company was sold up, leaving him without work when the spectre of mass unemployment was looming on the horizon of the post-war economic boom. Nor was there any hope of going back into football – unless the authorities could be persuaded to lift their ban on him.

An answer came from Huddersfield, where the Town Football Club were looking for an assistant to their secretary-manager Ambrose Langley, who had partnered Chapman's brother at Hull before the war. Chapman's impressive record at Northampton and Leeds – and the fact that he was out of work – made him an ideal choice. He was approached by the Huddersfield directors early in 1921 and the offer spurred him on to a determined effort to prove his innocence in the Leeds City affair. The Football League were finally swayed by the argument that because Chapman was absent from Leeds City at the time of the alleged illegal payments, he could not have known about them. They gave their permission for his appointment at Huddersfield Town. The news went unreported in the Press, so quickly had Chapman become football's forgotten man.

Huddersfield Town had experienced a mixture of success and near-disaster in its relatively short life. Nine years after entering the League in 1910, and shortly after the dissolution of Leeds City, the Town went through a financial crisis so serious that it was proposed to transplant the club to the vacant site at Elland

Road, Leeds. But supporters responded well to a cash appeal and when J. G. Cock, the striker, was sold to Chelsea for £2,500 the continuance of the club in Huddersfield was assured. In 1920 they were promoted to the First Division and got to their first Cup final, against Aston Villa at Stamford Bridge, where they were beaten 1–0.

Chapman brought to his new job his already extensive experience of industrial management, and Langley, reading between the lines, realized that such a dynamic personality would not remain an assistant for long. Only a month after Chapman's arrival, Langley resigned and left for Sheffield where he took over a pub. William Barr, the trainer, departed with him and the new secretary-manager got John Chaplin, his former trainer at Leeds, to come from Bristol Rovers.

Chapman's first move was to tell his directors: 'You have talented, mostly young, players – they need a general to lead them. I know the man and I think we can get him.'[1] The man he had in mind was Clem Stephenson, the Aston Villa inside-forward who played for Leeds City during the war.

If Chapman had become football's forgotten man, he was about to put himself, and his new club, in the public eye again, for on 16 March, 1921 Huddersfield bought Stephenson for a fee that was 'probably the highest ever paid by a Yorkshire club' – £4,000. (The national record in 1921 stood at £4,600.) The *Yorkshire Evening News* described the deal as 'a rare stroke of business'. It had been known for some time that relations between Stephenson and Villa were strained because of the player's insistence on living in his home-town of Newcastle, and several clubs, keen to secure him, were watching the situation closely. Chapman, with perfect timing, anticipated events by arranging to meet Stephenson at Leeds, on his way home from Birmingham. The player was adamant that if he was to play for Huddersfield he must be allowed to live in Newcastle. Chapman agreed.

Stephenson, by now thirty-three, had joined Aston Villa in 1911 and soon established himself as a powerful forward. Strangely, his only international appearance was for the English against the Scottish League in 1914. He had a way of beating the offside trap of defenders like Newcastle's McCracken by waiting until the ball was in his own half of the field before attacking. He was an ex-miner, and this endeared him all the more to Chapman, who, being familiar with mining, knew and admired the strength and fighting qualities which life down the pit bred in a man.

The arrival of Stephenson revolutionized the Huddersfield side almost overnight. Performances improved noticeably and gates began to top the 20,000 mark. 'By his energy and enterprise,' Chapman had 'helped to bring the club into smoother waters, and put its affairs on a proper systematized basis,' said the *Huddersfield Daily Examiner*.

The Town was beginning to make news in other ways too. In April 1921 they were invited to play in Paris against the Olympic Club there, a Belgian side and then Clapton Orient, who would be in the French capital at the same time. It was Huddersfield's first overseas tour. Later, attempts were made, initially without success, to bring a Scottish team to Leeds Road for a match in aid of the Mayor's fund for the unemployed.

The French tour went ahead in May as planned, but with a game against Red Star, the French champions, instead of the Belgian team. The Huddersfield party arrived in Paris in the early morning after a journey of nearly twenty-four hours by train and boat, and spent the first day sightseeing. They beat Red Star 2–0 and Clapton Orient 1–0, and Chapman sent a jubilant telegram to the *Examiner* reporting that the team had also won a 'nice trophy', the Bronze Lion. It was Chapman's second foreign tour (after Northampton's German visit of 1909) and he became a firm advocate of overseas ventures, because of their publicity value and because they gave an opportunity of displaying the English soccer style to foreign audiences.

Back in Huddersfield, Chapman helped to form a third, junior team which in June 1921 entered the West Riding Amateur League. The move was necessary in part because the limited finances of the club, stretched by the buying of Stephenson, made impossible the large-scale buying of ready-made players at high transfer fees. The third team was put in the charge of Billie Balmer, a former Everton full-back, while Jack Foster, a former

Sunderland and Huddersfield centre-forward, was given the running of the reserves as well as acting as scout.

A proven judge of footballing talent, Chapman took great interest in the third team. He took particular care of young players, seeing that they were well-fed and well-lodged and that they sent some money home to their parents each week.

To give all his players better club conditions he persuaded his directors to spend money on improving dressing and recreation rooms, and before long he could boast that the Town's facilities were the best in the country.

As a break in pre-season training in August 1921, Chapman and his players went on a charabanc trip to Harrogate, where they enjoyed an afternoon game of bowls. At the same time the manager's efforts to arrange a Scottish fixture led to an invitation from a Glasgow sports journalist for Huddersfield to play in Scotland.

The match, against Clyde, was a benefit for Frank Thompson, the Irish international and former Bradford City half-back. It was played in October, and during their visit Chapman and his party went to Hampden Park and to the Glasgow Industrial Exhibition at Kelvin Park, as well as enjoying a sing-song at the Alhambra Music Hall. Huddersfield won their match 4–0.

The pre-season period also saw more improvements for players, reporters and public. The pitch was re-turfed, and the Press seats brought to the front of the stand, giving a better view. Terracing opposite the stand was enlarged to hold 24,000 spectators. And an indication of growing support was the much-improved sales of three-guinea season tickets, totalling £1,100. The reward for this support was Huddersfield's first FA Cup.

The 1922 Cup campaign started with a tough tie away to League champions Burnley. Training was at Blackpool and involved the usual walks, rounds of golf, and Turkish and tonic baths, as well as a trip to the theatre. Chapman's message to Huddersfield's supporters was full of his customary cheery confidence: 'The team are having a fine time. All are contented, happy, fit and well. Never have I seen a happier set of fellows, and with an equal share of luck we shall not be defeated on Saturday.' For seventy-five minutes, however, it looked as though luck had deserted them:

Burnley were two goals up. Then Huddersfield rallied, and the fiery centre-forward Islip forced his way through to beat the tiring Burnley defenders. Half a minute from time centre-half Tom Wilson equalized to earn a replay.

A crowd of more than 35,000 flocked to Leeds Road on the Wednesday afternoon and several workshops had to close down. One engineering firm had so many applications for time off that it warned absentees they would be suspended for three weeks. In a deluge of rain, Huddersfield won 3–2.

The next rounds saw two more replays at Leeds Road, against Brighton and Blackburn Rovers, with more mills and businesses closing for the afternoon. Then, with a win over Millwall, Huddersfield were in the semi-final, against Notts County at Turf Moor. County were beaten 3–1, but the omens did not look favourable when the Town's mascot, a stuffed donkey, caught fire at the post-match celebration. The flames were put out in good time and the donkey was said to be fit for the final, against Preston North End. It was a proud day for the Huddersfield manager. For the first time since the Southern League Championship of 1909 a major honour was within reach.

The run-up to the final was not encouraging. Since December, when Huddersfield were among the top four, League results had slumped, bringing the Town into the relegation zone. The team needed a confidence boost – and got one. On the Saturday before the final Preston came to Leeds Road for a League match and were beaten 6–0.

The result confirmed Huddersfield as favourites for the Cup. They had been in the final only two years before, whereas Preston's last appearance was in 1889.

The 1922 final, the third and last at Stamford Bridge, was dubbed the 'Battle of the Roses'. Huddersfield's jerseys carried the white rose of Yorkshire while Preston's sported the red of Lancashire. The game was certainly a battle, with no lack of foul play, and it was appropriate that it should be won by a penalty. Huddersfield's winger Billy Smith was felled on the edge of (some said just outside) the area, and he drove the ball home from the spot, despite the goalkeeper's efforts to distract him by jumping up and down. So it was that Huddersfield became the first club to win the Cup with a penalty.

An interesting feature of the game was the play of centre-half Tom Wilson. Traditionally, the centre-half, under the offside law as it then was, played chiefly as an attacker, but even before the offside law was changed in 1925 to increase goal-scoring chances, and thus bring about a need for stronger defence, he was becoming more a third defender. This was the part that Wilson largely took in the final, becoming a 'great spoiler', as the *Examiner* put it. Already the defending centre-half was developing as a vital pivot in the balance of attack and defence. It was the logical outcome of the tactics of drawing out opposing defenders originally outlined by Chapman at Northampton. The change in the offside law, when it came, was merely the catalyst, not the sole cause, which produced the 'stopper'.

The rough play in the final, the last in an undistinguished post-war series, which all ended 1–0, inevitably led to recriminations. The FA, which usually refrained from comment on its Cup finals, was led to express its 'great regret' at the behaviour during the game, and hoped that 'there will not be any similar conduct in any future Final tie'. Huddersfield asked the FA to name names, but they declined and rebuked the club for not recognizing misbehaviour when they saw it.

The bickerings were forgotten in the scenes of wild excitement that greeted the Cup in Huddersfield. In London the winners held their celebration dinner at the Hotel Great Central, Marylebone, where Chapman praised the Town for carrying off a major prize while still relatively young (the club was founded in 1908). He said the secret of success was 'a happy team and a happy board of directors', one of the basic principles of his style of management. As if to underline this the players each received a gold watch to commemorate their Cup triumph, despite a loss for the year of £1,700.

A 29,000 crowd cheered as Chapman led his team onto the Leeds Road pitch on the Monday after the final for a League game against Middlesborough. The Cup was paraded round the ground at half-time, and Huddersfield won the match 2–1, to pull clear of the relegation zone. At a civic reception that evening Chapman announced that the club would not be satisfied until it had won the League Championship.

The season ended with a flourish. Huddersfield won the Charity Shield, beating the new champions Liverpool at Old Trafford, and in the last week of May the team left for a tour of Denmark. The new third team also augured well by winning the West Riding Cup and joining the Yorkshire Midweek competition, a move that provided better training grounds for the young players.

10

THE FIRST CHAMPIONSHIP HAT-TRICK

A measure of Chapman's success at Huddersfield was the support the club attracted. The country was in the grip of economic depression, and in June 1921 there were more than two million out of work. And it was centres like Huddersfield, whose main industries were mining, engineering and textiles, that suffered most. In these cities it was not unusual for half the working population to be jobless, while the wages of those in work – including professional footballers – fell. In 1921 the Football League lowered the maximum wage from £9 to £8.

The League also refused to allow concessions to unemployed supporters at the turnstiles. In October 1921 the Huddersfield unemployed sent a deputation to Herbert Chapman asking for admission charges (raised from 6d to 1s in 1919) to be waived or lowered for those with a dole card. Chapman told them it was not a decision that could be made by the club. Barrow, he said, had tried a concessions scheme but the League had banned it.

Despite this, the crowds kept coming to Leeds Road, drawn by the success Chapman had brought to the side. The ground became more accessible after June 1922 when Huddersfield Corporation started running buses direct to the south-west end.

Another factor in this growing support was the relegation of Bradford City, which left Huddersfield as the only centre of First Division soccer in the West Riding. This situation lasted for three years, until Leeds United were promoted in 1924.

Chapman's opening move in the quest for the League Championship was to sign a new goalkeeper. It was said that he always got the man a club didn't want to sell, but when he signed Ted Taylor from Oldham Athletic he got the man the club might not have wanted to sell. Chapman didn't want Oldham to know that

Taylor was the man he was after in case they refused to part with
him. Oldham had another 'keeper, a local lad whom, the wily
manager knew, the club really would be sorry to let go. So, to
be sure of his man, Chapman worked out his approach carefully.
He travelled to Oldham in a taxi with the Huddersfield director
Dick Parker. 'Suddenly,' Mr Parker recalled, 'he calmly turned to
me and said he would not negotiate for Taylor at all, would
pretend he knew nothing about him, and would go all out for the
other goalkeeper.' The ploy worked beautifully. The Oldham
directors resolutely refused to release their local man, and after
several hours of talks Chapman asked: 'All right, then, what about
this other chap Taylor?' Terms were agreed, and the Huddersfield
pair came away with the player they had wanted all along.

It was at this time that Chapman made another of his 'dis-
coveries'. He later remembered with special affection his signing
of George Brown, then seventeen, in his native village of Mickley,
Northumberland. After travelling to the little mining village and
speaking to Brown's mother, 'I then set out to find him, having
been told that he had gone to the pit with a barrow to fetch some
coal. I met a lad wheeling a barrow in the village street. "Are you
George Brown?" I asked.' He was, and when the youth heard
that Herbert Chapman wanted him to play for Huddersfield, 'I
remember how he dropped the barrow. In fact, he was so eager to
be off that he would have left it in the street if I had not insisted
that he should take the coals to his mother.'[1]

Brown went on to share Huddersfield's individual scoring record
in one season with 35 goals in 1926. In a seventeen-year career
with Huddersfield, Aston Villa, Leeds United and Darlington his
goal total reached 268. At Huddersfield he developed into an
expert practitioner of the art of inside passing, a tactic Chapman
had first encouraged at Northampton and preferred to long centres
from the wing. This frontal assault on goal, he explained to the
Examiner, was held to be a 'more deadly, if less spectacular,
method' than the 'senseless policy of running along the lines and
centring just in front of the goalmouth, where the odds are nine
to one on the defenders'.

Another inspired signing was centre-forward Charles Wilson

from Spurs. After his inclusion in the side the Town rose from seventeenth place to third, where they finished the season, their highest position yet. There was improvement too in the reserves, who finished fourth in the Central League, and the third team juniors won the Yorkshire Midweek League. But Huddersfield lost the Cup in a replay at Bolton, the Wanderers, with their graceful and deadly striker David Jack, going on to win the trophy in the first final to be played at Wembley. Huddersfield made up for their failure in the Cup by winning the League Championship in the next season, 1923-4.

The odds were often stacked against the Town's first League triumph. Injuries and sickness wiped out half the regular first team early in the season, and the goal-scoring burden fell disproportionately on the left-wing triangle of half-back Watson, Stephenson (now captain) and Smith. Despite this Huddersfield went to the top for one week in October, until a 1–1 draw at Liverpool, watched by prime minister Stanley Baldwin on his first visit to a football match. They didn't regain top place until April, after a winter that saw a home defeat by strugglers Chelsea and another 'flu epidemic. 'In these circumstances there is not much encouragement to lead one to believe that the team can re-assert their League claims very strongly,' commented the *Examiner*. But from April onwards it was obvious that either Huddersfield or Cardiff would win the Championship.

The final drama was played on 3 May, 1924, with Huddersfield home to Nottingham Forest and Cardiff away to Birmingham. For the Town to win the Championship, they needed to win and Cardiff to lose or draw. Huddersfield got their win, and all attention turned to the result from Birmingham. It was, said the *Examiner*, 'an unusual sight to see the crowd hanging about after the match instead of rushing for the tramcars. The little room at the end of the paddock, where scores are received, became for once the centre of attraction.' In the room a small group waited anxiously by the telephone. 'Then suddenly the door was flung open and Mr Chapman dashed out with his face one huge smile and shouting "we've won!" ' Birmingham had held Cardiff to a goalless draw and Huddersfield were champions.

They became the first club since the war to win the Cup and the League, and were the first to win the League on goal average. The reserves were denied the honours in the Central League by the same process of calculation, but the third team won the Yorkshire Midweek League for the second year running.

The 1924 Championship finally established Chapman as one of the most famous figures in football. He was featured in the *Examiner's* series of 'Impertinent portraits' of distinguished local citizens and hailed, like Napoleon, as the 'organizer of victory':

'His have been the brains behind the team, his the directing skill that has paved the way to success. Town is on everyone's lips today, and for the proud position which it occupies in public esteem it has very largely Mr Chapman to thank.'

Unfortunately, the season had not passed without a black mark against Huddersfield's reputation. A goalless draw against newly-promoted Notts County at Leeds Road in September 1923 was afterwards described by the *Examiner* as 'one of the most disgraceful exhibitions ever seen under the auspices of the Football Association'. The trouble started with a violent clearance by the Notts full-back Cope, and continued with an argument between Islip and Notts' other full-back Ashurst. Islip was sent off after bringing down the goalkeeper Iremonger (they were 'probably two of the most hot-headed players in the League,' said the *Examiner*), then Flint of Notts County was also sent off for attacking Smith. There were fouls galore, and the Town, to their credit, admitted the disgrace: 'If what we served up on Saturday is football, well, the sooner its death knell is sounded the better; may we go further and say that never do we wish to see anything like it again.' The club asked the FA for an inquiry, which was held at Sheffield, with Chapman attending. Islip and Flint were suspended for a month, and Iremonger 'severely censured'.

Chapman, incensed that anyone could sully the good name of Huddersfield, arranged for Islip's transfer to Birmingham, at an undisclosed fee said to be 'staggering'.

While Chapman's team first reached the top of the table, in October 1923, a petition was sent to the FA asking for the ban on his former colleagues at Leeds City to be lifted. The FA turned down the request and repeated its demand to see the Leeds City books. For Chapman, however, the Leeds affair was in the dim and distant past as he steered Huddersfield Town to a second League Championship. In the close season of 1924 he signed outside-right John Williams from Rotherham at a 'dirt cheap' price of under £2,000. Williams gave greater poise to the right flank, correcting the imbalance in the forward line which put too much weight on the left wing. Like Fanny Walden, he was a small player who could upset opponents by sheer pluck combined with skill, and he soon became a popular figure at Leeds Road.

A novelty for the home crowd at reserve matches in 1924-25 was music from gramophone records broadcast through a loudspeaker. An early programme included excerpts from *Il Trovatore,* a march by the Coldstream Guards Band and advertisements read by an announcer, including facts about 'certain unnoticed qualities in beef juices'.

A novelty of another kind came in October when Billy Smith became the first player to score direct from a corner kick in the 4–0 home defeat of Arsenal. The law governing corners had been amended earlier in the year to allow such goals.

Huddersfield began the season well, but lost the leadership in October. They regained it in February, clinching the Championship outright this time, with a draw at Notts County, while the reserves won the Central League. For the last match, at home to Liverpool, the Town players took the field as the band played 'See the Conquering Hero Comes', and were showered with streamers and confetti. The League and Central League trophies, for the first time held by one club, decked with blue and white ribbons, were displayed in the directors' box and carried round the field at half-time.

Chapman had put the Town on a firm footing that would see them to a third championship the following year to become the first club to win the title three years in succession; and two years after that they were runners-up. He had made Huddersfield a great club, and in so doing established himself as a unique figure, the first of the modern soccer managers. All the hallmarks of his management policy, that were to bring such outstanding results at

Arsenal, were there at Huddersfield.

Everyone connected with the club was encouraged to pull together as one big family, and Chapman fostered the spirit of co-operation by consulting his directors on team matters and winning the confidence of the players. 'No club in the country develops the get-together spirit more deliberately than the Champions, and the records show how the policy pays,' observed the *Sporting Chronicle*. But there was no doubt as to Chapman's overall control. He had the last word, and everyone looked to him as the brains behind Huddersfield's phenomenal success. He was, as the *Examiner* put it, the 'Napoleon of football', and 'probably no manager has more power from the team selection standpoint'. He made the players feel they belonged to a great club, where even playing in the reserves was all part of an important and worthwhile enterprise. And the team talks he had first started at Leeds heightened their sense of involvement. Chapman's appreciation of individual strengths and weaknesses meant that each man was played in the position that best suited and developed his talents. The approach was one of human understanding. 'It was Chapman's tact that won the players over to him,' says Dick Parker. 'He would always listen to a player's problems and offer help where he could. He had no qualms about dropping players he thought were off form, but would talk to them individually to encourage them, or if he wanted to make a point arising from their game. He never spoiled, nor allowed others to spoil, his players with too much praise, but struck a subtle balance between encouragement and discipline.'

As the Huddersfield *Year Book* for 1925-26 put it, he controlled his men in a 'firm but kindly manner'. In addition, he saw to it that the players had decent changing-rooms, and 'expert and scientific training methods' to 'preserve and lengthen their careers' (*Examiner*).

Such understanding was – by tradition – absent at other clubs. When Sir Matt Busby was playing in Manchester City's third team, the manager would say only: ' "You will have to get sharp away." They were the only words ever spoken to me as a player that could remotely be termed coaching . . . nobody realized that a young player needed reassurance.'[2] At Spurs, amateur centre-forward Billy Jones found the same aloofness in the manager: 'He stayed in his office most of the time. We hardly ever saw him. The trainer took daily charge of the team, and on match days the manager just sat in the stand. His name was McWilliam. I can't even remember his Christian name.' (It was Peter, a former Newcastle player who later became an Arsenal scout.) 'Herbert Chapman had supreme control, unlike other managers then. What he said was law, like Brian Clough today.'[3]

Chapman stuck to his policy of going only for top-class players, for he knew the crowds would come to watch stars like Clem Stephenson and Charles Wilson, and with Huddersfield's limited supply of soccer enthusiasts it was essential to use every means to attract them.

Ground improvements and publicity were used for the same purpose, and so that football should reach as wide a public as possible, Chapman persuaded the *Examiner* to publish a Saturday sports edition, the first issue of which appeared on 10 January, 1925.

Above all, crowds came to watch Huddersfield because of the exciting football they played. It had all the characteristics of the Chapman style – swift, direct, efficient. Full-back Wadsworth's 'remarkable accuracy' turned defence immediately to attack by the way he could 'take the ball from an opposing forward and send it to the forward he thinks will make the best use of the pass' (*Examiner*). Long, low passes confused the most dogged defences to create scoring chances. At a time when goals generally were becoming rarer as the old offside tactics became more widespread, Huddersfield still gave the crowd plenty of them. As the *Examiner* observed, the 'low passing and the long-field play of the Leeds Road team has become famous in the football world'.

Famous too was Chapman's assessment of talent in young players, whom he would watch after reading weekly reports from his four scouts. The *Examiner* spoke of his 'ability to discover players who will earn laurels for themselves and their club; indeed, his discrimination in the capture of budding players has been described as uncanny'.

Nevertheless, getting youngsters to adopt a professional attitude was not always easy, as Chapman explained to a local young people's society in November 1924. When he thought he had signed one player, he had a letter from him saying, 'Dear Sir, I don't think I shall bother to turn out tomorrow.' In his talk Chapman also stressed the importance of good crowd behaviour. He wanted to see more 'young ladies' at matches because he thought they would 'raise the tone of supporters generally'. And he again attacked barracking: 'Bad language, gambling and barracking are the chief evils of the game. Professional players, like artists, are highly strung and affected by ill-considered "criticism" from the crowd.'

Chapman valued good sportsmanship highly, and still liked to be a good sport himself. In the summer of 1923 he turned out at inside-right for the local police in their fixture against the lawyers. Sadly, the forty-five-year-old's rotund physique proved too much and he was forced to retire for an early bath.

At Huddersfield Chapman had amply demonstrated his skilled diplomacy in getting players for the club, as in the signing of Stephenson and Taylor. Once he had decided on his man he moved in with a determination that usually beat the carefully-laid plans of other interested clubs, often to dramatic effect. The story of how Harold Dennis, an outside-left from Newark, came to play for Huddersfield was told by the *Worksop Guardian*.

Worksop were keen to sign the player. They 'had a motor car placed at their disposal . . . and planned to arrive at Dennis' home [at Ancaster, near Sleaford] at 9.30, so as to have a glass that cheers, and then talk until midnight, the earliest time for signing. They duly arrived at 9.30 in spite of torrential rain, wind, vivid lightning and unusually severe thunder.

'But they counted without the cleverness of Herbert Chapman. . . . He arrived at three o'clock, and by 3.20 Dennis was in Mr Chapman's motor car en route to the home of the League Champions.'

Dennis had earlier said he would love to go to the Worksop club.

More drama was to come in May 1925, when Chapman signed Alex Jackson, the Aberdeen winger, at nineteen one of the youngest internationals ever to appear for Scotland. Jackson was restless at Aberdeen and had ambitions to play in England, but he threatened to return to America, where he had lived earlier, if he was not released. Several English clubs were waiting to step in, but Chapman outwitted them all. He was determined to get Jackson, to give poise to the Town's still unsettled right wing. In his favour was Jackson's own desire to play for Huddersfield, but Everton and Liverpool were ready with offers.

The matter seemed settled when Chapman, after befriending the Aberdeen chairman, went to Hampden Park to watch Aberdeen play Queen's Park. At a nearby hotel next morning a binding offer was made for Jackson's transfer to Huddersfield. But then Sunderland came up with a new offer and Liverpool launched a fresh diplomatic offensive. According to the *Glasgow Daily Chronicle,* Liverpool officials, 'by a curious coincidence', went to a junior cup tie at Parkhead, Glasgow, which was being watched by a group from Aberdeen that included Jackson. The Anfielders did not have permission to approach the player, but this was granted at a dinner with the Aberdeen party that evening. They were quite unaware that Herbert Chapman, two hundred miles away in Huddersfield, knew what was going on. At 10 o'clock, as Jackson walked past Sauchiehall Street Station, a stranger spoke to him and led him away. Two amateur detectives followed them, but lost the trail. The player was then reported missing.

Jackson had been put up at a boarding house, to await the arrival of Herbert Chapman next morning. 'How Mr Chapman got to know what had happened in 12 hours is a mystery to some people, for he was in Huddersfield when the Liverpool deputation had bade goodnight to their hosts from Aberdeen. Nothing had seemed more certain than that Alex Jackson would be in Liverpool football next season.'

Chapman went with Jackson to visit the player's family at Renton, where he 'magnetized the old people with the charm of his personality'. It was there that Jackson signed for Huddersfield, at a transfer fee of £2,500.

Chapman was never to manage his most illustrious capture. On

11 May, 1925 the following advertisement appeared in *The Athletic News*:

ARSENAL FOOTBALL CLUB

is open to receive applications for the position of

TEAM MANAGER

He must be fully experienced and possess the highest
qualifications for the post, both as to ability and
personal character.
Gentlemen whose sole ability to build up a good
side depends on the payment of heavy and exhorbitant [*sic*]
transfer fees need not apply.

The advertisement was a formality. Arsenal asked Chapman to take the job and made an irresistible offer. He had created successful teams in the relatively small soccer centres of Northampton, Leeds and Huddersfield, but the potential support from the vast population of London gave infinitely greater scope. A move to the capital would give his two teenage sons greater career prospects. And Arsenal were offering an unusually high salary for a football manager – £2,000. The Huddersfield directors tried to persuade Chapman to stay, even offering him a salary to match Arsenal's. But nothing could now keep Chapman and London apart.

11

IN COMMAND

Chapman's prediction that it would be five years before Arsenal won a major honour was not only, with hindsight, amazingly accurate; it was also meant to be realistic. For when Chapman arrived in 1925 the Gunners were finding First Division survival a hard struggle.

Founded by munition workers at Woolwich Arsenal in 1886, the club enjoyed moderate success in the next decade, playing in the all-red shirts originally donated by Nottingham Forest. As amateurs, they won the Kent Senior Cup in 1890 and the London Senior Cup the next year. In 1893 they changed their name from Royal Arsenal to Woolwich Arsenal, adopted professional status and were elected to the Second Division. The following year their home was established at the Manor Ground, Plumstead, and in 1904 the club won promotion to the First Division. From then on fortunes took a downward turn: the Plumstead ground was situated in a remote corner of the capital and attendances were low. Then, in 1913, the new chairman, Sir Henry Norris, negotiated the removal of the club to Highbury, in the more populous area of North London.

It was an audacious move. Indeed, Bob Wall believes that 'in many ways this was the most astute single decision ever taken by the club.'[1] That, however, was in the long run. The immediate aftermath was relegation, with the lowest number of points (18) and goals (26) ever recorded by a First Division club.

After the Great War Sir Henry, an estate agent and former Mayor of Fulham, used his influence to get his club elected to the enlarged First Division, but Arsenal found it hard going, their best season being 1920-21 when they finished ninth. In 1924 they narrowly missed relegation.

The club was the victim of dissension at the top which permeated down to the players and sapped their confidence: the familiar malaise among clubs under the old style of management. At Highbury the trouble stemmed from the Canute-like attempts of Sir Henry Norris to halt the rising tide of transfer fees. He forbade his manager, Leslie Knighton, to spend more than £1,000 on a player, at a time when £3,000 or more was normal. The chairman, whose authority was supreme, was sure that the players Arsenal already possessed could, if properly deployed, produce a winning combination. So the side was constantly reshuffled, no player remaining in any position long enough to find his form. Team spirit was undermined.

Prejudice against small players led to another 'edict' from the chairman: he instructed his manager to buy no player under five feet eight inches tall. Knighton defied him by signing 'Midget' Moffat from Workington. Moffatt was transferred to Luton and Knighton resigned.

To fill the vacant position, Sir Henry, still nursing ambitions for the club he had guided and invested in for so long, wanted no one else but the outstandingly successful manager of Huddersfield Town. The approach was made, Chapman accepted – and team control passed from the amateur chairman to the professional manager.

Sir Henry Norris was an archetype of the old-style football club chairman, combining a slight knowledge of the game with a great deal of money to put into it, and he fitted the popular image with a walrus moustache that quivered when he was angry, and a pincenez that had the disconcerting effect of partially obscuring the direction of his gaze. But by taking Chapman on board he accepted the limitation of his own authority. For Chapman was successful – there was no arguing with that simple fact. And the chairman was won over by the manager's charm, powerful persuasiveness and dynamism.

The veto on transfer fees over £1,000 was forgotten. Almost as soon as he arrived at Highbury Chapman persuaded his chairman that the team needed Charlie Buchan, the long-shining star of Sunderland who, at thirty-four, was seen as the man to inspire and lend experience to the faltering Arsenal attack. Sunderland wanted £4,000 and their manager, Bob Kyle, said it would be worth it for the twenty goals Buchan was bound to score in his first season at Highbury. The money-conscious Sir Henry seized on this point and suggested a £2,000 fee plus £100 for every goal Buchan scored in the next twelve months. The deal was agreed, and the novelty of the terms put Arsenal in the headlines as never before.

The son of a Scottish blacksmith who had moved south from Aberdeen, Buchan had played for Arsenal as an amateur in the Woolwich days, until he presented an expenses bill for 11s, and was suspended for extravagance. In 1911, after playing professionally for the Southern League side Leyton, he was bought by Sunderland for £1,200. He first met Chapman when he played a game for Leeds City in 1917. The next meeting came when Chapman called at the player's sports shop in Sunderland to ask him if he would agree to move to Arsenal. At first Buchan thought he was joking, and had to telephone his manager to get confirmation that his club had agreed to the transfer. He recalled in his autobiography: [2]

'Slowly, I put down the receiver. I was almost stunned by what I had heard. It had never crossed my mind that Sunderland would be prepared to part with me so easily.'

Buchan said he would think it over, and agreed to the move when Chapman called back again next day. ' "Will you give me your word you'll sign?" he asked; and when I replied "Yes", we talked of other things. A lot of them concerned the Arsenal team and what I thought about them.'

Sir Henry Norris's old transfer limit was broken again with the buying of Bill Harper, Hibernian's international goalkeeper, for £5,000. A former blacksmith and heavyweight boxing champion in the Scots Guards, Harper won several Scottish caps in the home internationals of 1923 to 1925.

But the chairman's readiness to provide the cash for Chapman's shopping was to prove his downfall. An obstacle to Buchan's transfer was that he would lose income from his Sunderland shop, and the deal was delayed for two months while 'under-the-counter' terms were agreed to compensate him for this loss. This was to come to light two years later when the Football Association appointed a commission to inquire into allegations that Sir Henry had offered financial inducements above the legal fees to attract players to Highbury and that he had diverted club funds to his private account. The commission found him guilty, and he and a fellow director were forced to resign.

When the *Daily Mail* published the commission's findings, Norris took legal action against the paper, then dropped it in favour of a libel suit against the FA, to challenge the suggestion that he had acted dishonestly.

The case, heard in February 1929, revealed that, since his association with Arsenal began in 1910, Sir Henry had placed some £15,000 of his own money at the club's disposal (a bounty which could explain his campaign against rising transfer fees). After more than ten years he decided that it was time he retrieved some of the money, so from 1921 to 1923 he put the wages of his chauffeur on Arsenal's expense account and in 1926 charged the club £125 for hiring, over two years, a motor car. During the hearing, he claimed that Chapman and the directors knew of this and accused the manager of lying when he told the commission he did not know. And his defence maintained that the FA had a grudge against him because he had openly criticized the transfer system. Sir Henry said he wanted the money for the car hire as repayment for the £125 he paid to Buchan as compensation for the loss of his sports shop. Chapman, he said, had begged him not to let Buchan go, but at the same time made it clear that, because of his previous suspension for alleged financial irregularities at Leeds in 1919, he preferred not to have anything to do with extra payments. Asked why, knowing that such practices were illegal yet widespread, he had not made a stand against them, Sir Henry replied: 'Because we should not have got the players.'

The court upheld the FA's verdict and Sir Henry left football for good. His successor at Arsenal, Sir Samuel Hill-Wood, was content to leave Chapman with a free rein to work out his grand designs. The manager's rule was now complete, a state of affairs that has continued ever since. Writing in 1969, Bob Wall says:

'One hears a great deal about interference from boards of directors in football and of managers not being allowed a free hand to run their teams. That charge certainly cannot be levelled at Arsenal. Our chairman, Mr Denis Hill-Wood [son of Sir Samuel], put it succinctly when he discussed the board's role with me a number of years ago. "Why pay experts to do a job if non-experts are going to be allowed to interfere?" he asked.'[3]

So Herbert Chapman established a pattern in relations between directors and manager which has become a feature of many of the major clubs, where the only veto on the manager's power is the sack if he fails to bring results.

12

THE TEAM TAKES SHAPE

It was not only Sir Henry Norris who was won over by Chapman's infectious optimism. When the new manager arrived at Highbury he made administrative changes which deprived Arsenal's fifty voluntary workers – mostly schoolteachers acting as stewards and programme sellers – of various perks. When the crowds had left after the second home match, Chapman met the helpers in the stand and asked them to take him on trust, asserting that the changes were in the club's interest. Years later he could report that 'we still have our fifty voluntary workers'.

Having installed himself and his family in a comfortable, modern house in Hendon, Chapman spelled out his aims in the programme for the first match. They were 'to make Arsenal Football Club one of the best football clubs from all points of view' and to 'employ, without exception, the very best type of player to represent the club . . . above all, he must be a gentleman both on and off the field; he must be a clever player, who can think out attractive, constructive tactics; and he must be wholeheartedly enthusiastic and keen to make progress in the game.'

Buchan fitted the bill perfectly; he was an experienced, thoughtful player who was always seeking to improve his performance and working out moves for the next game. The delay in his transfer over his sports shop confirmed Chapman's estimation of him, for he admired players who sought to protect their own interests: 'This is an indication to me that the player who makes this demand has intelligence.'[1]

Buchan scored 21 goals in his first season, giving Sunderland another £2,100 under the transfer terms, £100 more than they had originally asked for. Chapman switched Jimmy Brain from inside-forward to centre-forward to create a powerful new source

9 Clem Stephenson.

10 Alex James and Cliff Bastin.

1 Charlie Buchan.

12 David Jack in action at the 1930 Cup final.

13, 14 The 1930 Cup final. *Left*: King George V meets the Arsenal players. *Right*: Tom Parker carries off the Cup.

15 Arsenal's Cup-winning team. *L. to R. back*: Baker, Lambert, Preedy, Seddon, Hapgood, John; *middle*: Chapman, Jack, Parker, James, Whittaker; *front*: Hulme, Bastin.

of goals, for Brain went on to score 31 that season, breaking the club's individual record. The position of Bob John was stabilized at left-back, Billy Blyth was recalled to form the 'three Bs' half-back line with Baker and Butler, and Dr Jimmy Paterson, the amateur outside-right, was persuaded to make a comeback.

Chapman's opening campaign soon hit disaster. In October 1925 Arsenal were defeated 7–0 at Newcastle. Buchan, in the heat of the moment, threatened to leave the club after such a humilia-tion so near his old Sunderland home. Characteristically, how-ever, Chapman was to learn from the defeat, just as he had done twenty years before after Northampton's defeat by Norwich. The result was a new combination which was to put Arsenal on top of the football world – and to change the course of soccer history.

The goal deluge at St James's Park brought home the need to counter the effects of the new offside law which came into force that summer and which reduced from three to two the number of players required to be between an opposing attacker and goal when the ball was last played. The change was aimed at reducing stoppages for offside, which in the 1920s were the cause of much monotony as full-backs played further and further upfield. The revised law opened the scoring floodgates. In the last season before its introduction, 4,700 goals were scored in the League; during the next season the number went up to 6,373.

Chapman realized that to survive a team now needed three instead of two full-time defenders to cover the gap in the centre of the field. Centre-halves had always played defensively at times, but now their role was to become primarily defensive. So centre-half Jack Butler was given the job of staying by the penalty area to break down opposing attacks, helped by the full-backs marking opposing wingers and the wing-halves the opposing inside-forwards. Defence-in-depth had begun.

Chapman took the defensive centre-half idea from a suggestion by Buchan, and it was Buchan who proposed another tactical innovation. Pulling the centre-half back left a gap in midfield which needed a link man to pick up passes from defence and lay them on for the forwards. Buchan offered himself for the job, but Chapman valued him as a goalscorer, and the link-man role went to Andy Neil. The other forwards were told to go fast, like 'flying columns', round the slow, old-style defences and if possible to make for goal direct. It was a style of forward play Chapman had adopted at Northampton Town, based on long, low passing and direct assault.

The new tactics were drawn up quickly: two days after the Newcastle débacle Arsenal went to West Ham and won 4–0. To boost the team's performance Chapman recalled veteran winger Jock Rutherford, then over forty, who had begun his League career with Newcastle in 1901. From Blackburn Rovers he signed outside-right Joe Hulme, said to be the fastest footballer in the game and famed for his accurate centres while running. Blackburn Rovers had paid York £250 for Hulme, but he cost Arsenal £3,500. He was an all-round sportsman, playing cricket for Middlesex and excelling at golf, table tennis and snooker.

Arsenal finished the 1925-6 season as League runners-up with 52 points, five behind hat-trick champions Huddersfield, in the highest position ever reached by a London club (Arsenal's previous best was sixth in 1909). Profits from gate receipts were £6,500, another club record. And while goals for stood at 87 – almost double the previous season's total, goals conceded went up by only five, to 63.

That summer, as the country went through the turmoil of the General Strike, Chapman took his players on a tour of Europe – and nearly spent a night in a Paris jail. There was a mix-up over payment for a meal at a café, and Chapman was hauled off by a gendarme to the police station. The embarrassing affair was eventually sorted out and he was released.

Chapman strengthened his squad by buying Charlie Jones from Nottingham Forest. Jones, a Welsh international who impressed the Arsenal manager with his fighting qualities and intelligent play, was to be the 'flying-column' on the left-wing, matching Hulme on the right. Then came inside-forward Jack Lambert, 23, costing £2,000 from Doncaster Rovers and like Baker, John and Brain a former miner. With Buchan inspiring the attack, right-back Tom Parker was bought from Southampton to give similar leadership to the defence, and was made captain.

After the successes of 1925-6, the team suffered from over-confidence and performances were disappointing. Butler couldn't adapt to his new defensive role, and Chapman began to look around for a more solid defender, not necessarily a player with much technical skill, but one who could clear accurately under pressure, feeding the ball to an inside-forward. In December he found Herbie Roberts, 21, an amateur wing-half from Oswestry, who cost a mere £200. The defensive headers of the tall, red-haired Roberts soon made him a familiar figure at Highbury, and he was the first defending centre-half to earn the name 'policeman' or 'stopper'. His clearances to midfield turned defence immediately to attack. They were taken up by the fast-running forwards to outplay and outwit the slow and often clumsy defensive play of oppositions who had failed to grasp the significance of the changed offside rules. Speed was the essence of the system.

In 1927 Chapman added finesse to Arsenal's defence by buying full-back Eddie Hapgood – a former milkman – from Kettering Town. He was nineteen, and had been rejected by his home-town club, Bristol Rovers. He was to prove one of Chapman's finest bargains. With his calm, smooth tackling and impeccable conduct on the field, Hapgood was to become one of the ablest and most respected players ever to captain Arsenal and England. Bob Wall says of him:

'He played his football in a calm, authoritative way and he would analyse a game in the same quiet, clear-cut manner. Eddie set Arsenal players the highest possible example in technical skill and personal behaviour.'[2]

A non-drinker and non-smoker, Hapgood's only addiction was physical fitness. He was also a vegetarian, although the story goes that Chapman persuaded him to eat steaks after hearing that he sometimes felt faint when heading a ball. The thirty-six-patch leather ball of those days was heavy, and headers had to be strictly from the forehead. Anywhere else on the head, and even the strongest player could be knocked unconscious.

With the team still taking new shape, Arsenal reached the Cup final for the first time in 1927, their opponents being Cardiff City, one of the more successful sides of the decade. City were runners-up to Huddersfield in the League in 1924 and losing Cup finalists the following year. The team they fielded in the 1927 final included eight internationals. But Chapman's team-building made Arsenal the favourites.

Contrary to normal practice, 'the most discussed football official of recent years', as the *Daily Mail* described him, had his team training at Highbury in the week before the final, rather than at a country or seaside resort (Brighton was later to become the favoured Cup training ground). 'The men are not deviating by one hair's breadth from the ordinary system of training,' he told the *Daily News*. 'To alter that system, even for a Cup final, would be folly, and for that reason we think there is no place like home and Highbury for keeping the minds and bodies of our players in perfect tune.'

In goal for Arsenal was Welshman Dan Lewis, displacing Bill Harper, and Butler was back at centre-half in place of Roberts. In the Wembley dressing-room on the day, as the 92,000 crowd sang 'Abide with Me' in the newly-introduced programme of community singing, the players donned their new football shirts. The shirts were presented for the occasion by Buchan – and they were to be Arsenal's downfall. After seventy-three minutes of a disappointingly dull game, Lewis pounced on a shot by Cardiff's Ferguson only to find that the sheen of his new jersey caused the ball, with its polished leather, to slip from under him towards goal. He tried to stop it but succeeded only in propelling it across the line. He told the *Daily Mail* later:

'I got down to it and stopped it. I can usually pick up a ball with one hand, but as I was laying over the ball, I had to use both hands to pick it up, and already a Cardiff forward was rushing down on me. The ball was very greasy. When it touched Parker it had evidently acquired a tremendous spin, and for a second it must have been spinning beneath me. At my first touch it shot away over my arm. I sent my hand after it and touched it. I may have sent it quicker over the goal line with this touch, but I think it would have reached it in any case.'

This, perhaps the most tragic of all goals seen at Wembley, sent the Cup out of England for the first and last time. Lewis was so

upset by accusations that he had let his fellow Welshmen win that
his immediate reaction was to vow never to play again.

Total receipts for the final were £21,000; as a comparison with
more modern times, receipts for the 1976 final totalled £420,000.

Runners-up in the League and then in the Cup – there remained
only three more years for Chapman to complete his five-year plan.
Buchan, nearly 37, was approaching the end of his playing days,
and in 1928 left to become a sports reporter. To replace him,
Chapman decided to go for David Jack of Bolton Wanderers, the
England inside-forward. Famed for his grace and artistry, Jack
played in the first Wembley Cup final in 1923 and again three years
later. Bolton had made it clear that Jack was not for sale, but
Chapman, who in twenty years of football management rarely
failed to get his man, was determined.

It was said of him that he always got the player that a club
didn't want to sell, and the Jack transfer was a classic case in
point. He finally persuaded Bolton to sell, but the asking price was
an unprecedented £13,000, twice the previous record. A week
later, after two more meetings, the Bolton management was invited to London and entertained at the Euston Hotel. Bob Wall,
engaged in his first big transfer deal at Arsenal as Chapman's
assistant, takes up the story:

'We arrived at the hotel half an hour before our appointment.
Chapman immediately went into the lounge bar. He called the
waiter, placed two pound notes in his hand and said: "George.
This is Mr Wall, my assistant. He will drink whisky and dry ginger.
I will drink gin and tonic. We shall be joined by guests. They will
drink whatever they like. But I want you to be careful of one
thing. See that our guests are given double of everything, but Mr
Wall's whisky and dry ginger will contain no whisky and my gin
and tonic will contain no gin."

'When the Bolton pair arrived, Chapman ordered the drinks.
We quickly downed ours and he called for the same again. The
drinks continued to flow and our guests were soon in gay mood.

'Finally, when Chapman decided the time was opportune for
talking business, they readily agreed to letting him sign Jack –
and for £10,890, which we considered a bargain.

'Never did ginger ale and tonic water leave two persons so
elated. When we were safely in our taxi on the return journey to
Highbury, Chapman exclaimed: "Well, that's your first lesson in
football. You now know how to conduct a transfer." ' [3]

Jack, 29, had proved a hard bargainer himself – which raised
him even higher in Chapman's estimation. He was well aware
of his rights in a transfer, as his father was manager of Plymouth
Argyle. When Chapman called at Jack's house for his consent, the
player demanded various concessions and phoned his father for
advice. The Jack transfer was the first to command a five-figure
fee, despite the fact that Arsenal were continuing to propose limits
on transfer fees, which led to accusations of hypocrisy. Chapman
genuinely believed that, in the interest of the game, fees should be
limited, but while the proposals went unheeded he was quite prepared to spend as much as possible to secure the best players. For
he insisted that anything less was next to useless. He knew too that
Arsenal's resources, swollen from early successes, gave him a big
advantage in the transfer stakes: 'We can pay £2,000 more for a
player than any other club.' The critics, in labelling him a big
spender, also ignored his ability to spot bargains like Roberts and
Hapgood.

For Chapman, however, Jack was no less of a bargain, the record
fee a small price to pay for a player of his class. Looking back on
the deal, Chapman believed that 'one of the best bargains I ever
made was the most costly one.' Jack's début, on 20 October, 1928,
saw Arsenal's first victory at St James's Park for seventeen years,
when Newcastle were beaten 3–0.

The linking midfield role still needed to be filled. A number of
players had been tried, but none came up to the subtle demands
of the job. What was needed was a foraging inside-forward who
could pick up passes from defence and create scoring chances
for the other forwards. Chapman's search for the right man ended
in 1929 when Preston put on transfer at £9,000 their 'Wembley
Wizard' Alex James, the Scottish international who had been the
bane of England at Wembley the year before, when Scotland won
5–1. (A team-mate on that occasion was Alex Jackson, Chapman's
last signing at Huddersfield, who scored three of the five goals.)

In view of the nature of the job waiting for him, the buying of
James came as a surprise to observers. For this exuberant individualist revelled in the goal-scoring limelight and hardly seemed the
right choice for a midfield link man, laying on scoring chances for
others. Chapman was sure of his assessment, however; and though
James was just as fussy about the terms of his transfer as Jack
had been, he found the bright lights of the big city too attractive
a prospect to refuse Chapman's offer.

The final touch to the forward line came with seventeen-year-old
Cliff Bastin, costing £2,000 from Exeter City, who was to be
the last in a long line of Chapman discoveries that began with
Fanny Walden twenty years before. The manager spotted the
youngster at Watford, while checking on one of the home side's
players. He was struck by Bastin's cool, calculated style, and set
out hotfoot for Devon. Negotiations with Exeter, for whom
Bastin had signed professionally only weeks before, were successfully concluded, but Bastin himself, showing remarkable maturity
for his age, saw his training as an electrical engineer as a sounder
career prospect than Arsenal. He preferred the slow, peaceful life
of the Devon countryside to the frenetic bustle of the metropolis:
playing for Exeter seemed better than the likelihood of being very
small fish in the big Arsenal pool. Recalling his first meeting with
the Arsenal manager, whom he described as 'plump, rubicund
and genial', Bastin writes:

'There was an aura of greatness about Chapman. I was impressed by him straight away. He possessed a cheery self-confidence, which communicated itself to those around him. This
power of inspiration and the remarkable gift of foresight, which
never seemed to desert him, were his greatest attributes.' [4]

Chapman called at Bastin's home and tried to convince him of
the spectacular career he would have at Highbury. 'He cast me in
the role of a sort of footballing Dick Whittington, and took down
the vases from the mantelpiece to represent my stepping-stones to
fame,' Bastin recalls. At length, after consulting his mother, the
reluctant player finally agreed – on condition that he could continue with his electrical engineering studies.

The youngster's inclusion in the side earned him the name 'Boy

Bastin', as seventeen-year-olds in League football were much
scarcer than now, and Bastin was in a class of his own with the
fierceness of his shot, as a teaser of defences and as an expert
penalty-taker. The nickname stuck after 1930 when he became the
youngest player to appear in a Cup final, and by 1931, before his
twenty-first birthday, he had won Cup, Championship and international honours. (The pre-war record for the youngest player in
League football, incidentally, is held by Geldard of Bradford, who
was fifteen when he appeared in a Second Division match in 1929.)

Chapman now felt he had a team capable of winning something,
and he was determined that the 1929-30 season would be Arsenal's,
to keep his promise of five years before. Only Baker and John
remained as first team regulars from the pre-Chapman era, the
rest having been replaced at a cost of £40,000, the most prolific
spending spree soccer had seen.

The season began badly. League performances slumped disastrously, and there was even talk of relegation for the first time
since Chapman took over. His whole buying policy looked to be a
failure. James in particular, the man earmarked as the lynchpin in
the tactical plan, was not living up to expectations. Instead of
making chances for his colleagues, the Scot, as predicted, couldn't
get out of the habit of making for goal himself, so the attack was
stifled of passes.

In an effort to halt the slide, Chapman went to the Arsenal
purse again for £6,000 to buy David Halliday, Sunderland's prolific goalscorer. Halliday was planned for centre-forward, where
Brain, Lambert and Jack had all proved unsatisfactory. Bastin
was switched from inside- to outside-left, to become the left wing's
'flying column'. But when the Cup ties came round, Chapman
made another, more dramatic decision – he dropped Alex James,
the man intended as the team's dynamo, and sent him home for a
complete rest. Without him Arsenal beat Chelsea in the opening
round, but then faced a crisis when Birmingham forced a draw
at Highbury in the next round. Chapman's decision for the replay
was a master-stroke.

Only three days before the match he called at James's home,
and strode into the bedroom, where James was still in bed. 'Get up

Alex,' he said. 'You're coming to Highbury for training because you will be playing in the replay.' [5] He had calculated that a call to arms at such a short notice would bring out the fighting qualities in his ailing general – and it worked. Arsenal were through to the next round, and it was the turning point in the club's history. James displayed the long-awaited tactical skill needed to vitalize the team formation drawn up nearly five years before, and with Lambert finding new flair at centre-forward, one of the most famous attacking lines of all time had been forged. James's recall finally established the system of defence linked to attack by a midfield forager which was the key to the successes of the next decade. The Arsenal machine had been perfected, and the 1930 Cup triumph was to usher in a glorious future.

13

THE NAPOLEON OF NORTH LONDON

Chapman at Highbury was monarch of all he surveyed. At a time of economic depression, gates were booming as Arsenal's reputation for first-class entertainment grew, and profits reached £27,000 a year – a handsome sum for those days.

Like Napoleon, to whom he was often likened, Chapman was the organizer of victory. 'Breaking down old traditions, he was the first club manager who set out methodically to organize the winning of matches,' observed the *Daily Mail*. Most managers, before and since, have held the organizing of victory to be impossible. Bob Wall recalls: 'Chapman probably planned many of our wins. He would tell a player, "Never mind what the other team does – this is what you are going to do." He believed his tactics would win, regardless of how the opposition played. Sometimes it didn't work, but usually it did. Most managers today would say victory cannot be planned, and that all that is possible is to analyse the opposition. Chapman's approach was unique.'[1]

The approach was a reaction to the days when teams took the field without any overall plan of how they were to set about winning, when the only initiative that came from management was to encourage friendships in the team so that players were more ready to discuss tactics among themselves.

The team discussions Chapman introduced at Highbury played a big part in the planning of campaigns. At 9.30 on a Friday morning the players would arrive at the ground for training, then at mid-day would congregate in the manager's office to discuss the next day's match, as well as analysing the previous week's. Chapman, as we have seen, first held these sessions during his days at Leeds City, but now, instead of the diagram he used then, he had a magnetic table marked out as a football field, with little toy

players that could be moved around on it. With a detailed report
on the opposition at hand, everyone would give his views of the
game, suggest ideas and illustrate points of play. Gradually the
plan would be evolved, and the meeting would end with every
player fully aware of the role he was to play. 'I am convinced that
much of the success achieved by the Arsenal has been through the
team quickly sensing a weakness in the opposition,' Chapman
commented. This ability was sharpened by these players' meetings, which were a unique feature of football at this time. There
was no room for slackers: absolute concentration and dedication
throughout the game was demanded. It was one of Chapman's
rules that even when the ball was on the other side of the field, a
player must always be anticipating the next move.

The outpouring of so much mental energy on the planning of
victories often led Chapman to suffer acute anguish during a
game, for unlike Napoleon, he was powerless to lead his men once
battle had commenced.

It is an experience familiar to all great managers since. When
Arsenal met Hull in the Cup semi-final in 1930, and were 2–0
down with ten minutes to go, Chapman's ordeal on the bench grew
to a fever-pitch of intensity. 'So far as I knew I had attended to
every trifling detail, yet every plan, every hope, seemed to be
going wrong. I cannot tell you my thoughts as I sat on the stand
and watched the Arsenal playing far below their proper form. All
I was conscious of was that everything had miscarried, and in my
isolation, I was powerless to do anything. If only I could have
gone out there and helped to put matters right. Believe me, it is far
harder at such times to sit and look on than to be in the middle,'
he told *Sunday Express* readers.

Frank Cole of the *Daily Telegraph* wrote of Chapman: 'If you
sat near him at a big match ... you realized the intense earnestness
of the man. His face would go ashen grey as he lived every moment
of the play. And when things were going against his men he
seemed to be suffering mental agonies. I have never seen such concentration.'

Chapman's absolute authority over the team and his concern for
their performance on the field was highlighted by the firm rule

he laid down for match days. Former Arsenal and England full-back George Male recalls:

'The only people allowed in the dressing-room before a match were the eleven players, the boot man, the trainer and the manager. No player not appearing in that particular game dared put his face round the door. Even the chairman wasn't allowed to look in without Chapman's permission.'[2]

Similarly, at the weekly team talks, only the teams of the last and the coming match were admitted.

But it wasn't only the team over which Chapman held dominion. His official title (one used at most clubs) was secretary-manager, and as such the administration of the club was as much a part of his job as team management. (In later years, as paper-work increased, the two roles were separated, Bob Wall, Chapman's former administrative assistant, becoming secretary in 1956.) Wall recalls:

'No member of the staff was permitted to leave the building unless he had telephoned Chapman's office at six o'clock and enquired: "Is it all right for me to go now, Mr Chapman?"

'We all had a very great respect for him. I suppose too, there was a tinge or more of fear in our approach to him. We knew that jobs were not easy to obtain . . . we couldn't afford to risk getting the sack.

'Yet Chapman was a great man. If he put up a scheme, you would be willing to follow him to the ends of the earth to ensure its fulfilment. You always felt that what he said was right.

'He never thought of himself. Arsenal FC was his creed. He was a hard, yet scrupulously fair person to staff and players and he remained constant in his attitudes until he died.'[3]

In his showmanlike way, Chapman wanted Highbury to become the greatest club ground in the world, a new kind of foot-ball mecca, with a big crowd capacity and as futuristic in design as the new West Stand, built at his suggestion to replace the old wooden stand erected in 1913. The new stand was completed in November 1932 at a cost of £45,000 and formally opened the following month by the Prince of Wales. It was dedicated by the Reverend Norman Boyd, Chapman's vicar at St Mary's, Hendon, who acted unofficially as the club's chaplain. The stand contained 4,100 seats, installed at a cost of 2d each, and incorporated the latest in spectator comfort. In design it was the shape of things to come, the forerunner of the big, luxury stands at Goodison Park, Anfield, Stamford Bridge and other grounds of today.

Chapman also put in hand plans to cover the north terrace and rebuild the East Stand. Both schemes were realized after his death.

Another innovation made in 1932 was a huge 45-minute clock which Chapman had installed at the north end of the ground so that players and spectators could see at a glance how much time was left for play. It put him – not for the first time – on the wrong side of the Football Association, which saw the clock as undermining the referee's authority, and ordered its removal. Not to be denied, Chapman arranged a compromise in the form of a 24-hour clock, which remains, in its new position on the south bank, a familiar feature of Highbury.

Ground improvements were just one part of Chapman's plan to make Arsenal the most talked-about club in the kingdom. In 1932, he invited to his office a representative of the London Electric Railway to discuss the Piccadilly Line Underground station opposite the north end of the ground. Chapman had first appreciated the crowd-pulling potential of a station practically on Arsenal's doorstep, giving the club a quick connection with most parts of the capital, when he came to Highbury as the visiting manager of Leeds City in 1913, and it now fired his imagination. There was only one thing wrong – the name. Only the initiated knew that Gillespie Road was the stop for the Arsenal. The name had to be changed, but it would not be easy. The transport authorities did not alter the names of their stations lightly, because of the huge expense and inconvenience involved, including the reprinting of thousands of tickets, direction notices and maps. After a long preliminary chat with the man from the LER, Chapman decided it was time to press home the point. 'Whoever heard of Gillespie Road?' he exclaimed. 'This is Arsenal around here!' His visitor returned to his headquarters, the adjustments were made, and on 5 November, 1932, Arsenal arrived on the London transport network.

Another innovation connected with transport was for travel to away games. Journeys were usually made on the Friday, except for the relatively short trip to Birmingham, made on Saturday morning. In 1930 one of the railway companies was persuaded to reserve a carriage, with restaurant, exclusively for the club, this 'Arsenal carriage' being shunted onto the train for the journey. Novel, efficient and audacious, it was typical of Chapman's concern for his players' comfort. For as the carriage was always at the front or back, it could be kept private from the rest of the train. In more recent times, with motorways covering much of the country, the luxury coach, complete with colour television, is the preferred method of transport.

Nothing was left untouched where a change would put the club in the public eye, improve the team's performance or, preferably, both. The playing strip, for instance, underwent several changes. The colour of the team's socks, until 1927 black with thin red and white stripes, was altered to a more distinctive blue and white so that the players could recognize their colleagues more easily without looking up. Chapman favoured a red and white sock to match the club colours, but when this was tried the red dye ran when the socks were washed. It wasn't until 1970 that modern textile colouring made the now familiar red and white sock possible.

A more successful change was the abandoning of the coarse-knit, lace-up jersey in favour of a shirt with buttons at the neck and a turn-over collar. The new shirt appeared at the start of the 1932-3 season, with another, more startling change – white sleeves. By then, Chapman considered that the all-red jersey looked ordinary, out of tune with the club's distinction, so he decided that in line with Aston Villa, until then the club with the greatest prestige and tradition behind it, the sleeves should be of a different colour to the rest of the top.

Another experiment which, like the 45-minute clock, was nipped in the bud by the authorities, was the numbering of players. The idea was not new. It had been advocated countless times, but prejudice against it held sway, and it was argued that identifying players would pander to their individual egos. Then, in

August 1928, Arsenal took the field at Hillsborough wearing numbers on their backs, while on the same day, Chelsea, at home, were doing the same – at Chapman's suggestion. His view was that numbers would speed up moves by helping players identify each other more quickly, but the Football League was outraged and forebade a repeat. The intrepid manager had to content himself with numbering his reserve teams. Five years later the Football Association adopted numbering in the Cup final, using numbers 1 to 22, but Chapman was not finally vindicated until 1939 – five years after his death – when the League made it compulsory, primarily for the benefit of spectators.

Chapman's appetite for new ideas knew no bounds. 'I would borrow one from a programme boy at Highbury, if it were a good one,' he said. But he never made changes solely for their publicity value. He had a passionate concern for the welfare of football in general, and was always on the lookout for ways to make it more efficient, more attractive and more popular, although naturally he wanted Arsenal to be in the forefront. Some ideas he rejected, such as the liquid developed at Derby County for making pitches usable in all weathers. Accompanied by Bob Wall, he went to Derby during the harsh winter of 1933 to watch the solution being sprayed onto a corner of the pitch. The liquid dispersed the frost, but within an hour the ground was freezing again. Chapman was interested only in something that would last three hours.

The white football he regarded as another non-starter. Designed to counteract poor visibility on murky winter afternoons, it had been used in Scotland and by the visiting South Africans in 1924 before Arsenal adopted it for a public trial match three years later. Chapman could see no advantage in it and Buchan dismissed it as a 'stunt'. The manager sought a more effective answer to the frustrations and injustices caused by inadequate light in winter – floodlighting.

The early, nineteenth-century experiments in artificial lighting, including that held in Sheffield in the year of Chapman's birth, had been forgotten, and it was left to the Europeans to develop the idea of floodlit football. Chapman did not realize the possibilities until he visited Belgium in 1930 and watched a match played in Brussels during a thunderstorm:

'The field was illuminated by lights fixed to five standards running down one side behind the spectators. From each standard the rays of twenty powerful lamps were thrown across the pitch at different angles, and as they intersected and spread they did not leave a dark or even a dull patch. . . . I wished that the public at home could always have such a good view.'[4]

The players told him after the game that the lights did not trouble them as much as sunlight.

Later he visited Austria at the invitation of his friend Hugo Meisl, the Austrian team manager. After watching an international match, he was taken to a forest clearing where a game between two amateur sides was lit by car headlights. He became convinced of the future of floodlit football, and on arriving back at Highbury gave poor Bob Wall just one month to get hold of 'lanterns' for the practice ground. A railway company came to Wall's aid and before long a trial was held under floodlit conditions. Chapman saw that floodlighting, by enabling games to be played in the evening, would win people away from the rival attractions of dog racing ('it does not make the slightest appeal to me') and the speedway.

Despite the cold, he believed that people would be prepared to watch football at night. In any case, the cold could be overcome by heating the stands. He had floodlights built into the West Stand – but once again the FA stepped in.

The Association feared that if floodlighting caught on, clubs would be drawn into spending too much money, and it banned the new lights at Highbury from being used for official matches. For the rest of the decade they shone only on training sessions and ground maintenance work, and it was not until 1951, some twenty years after Chapman's enthusiastic advocacy, that the first official floodlit match was held, between Southampton and Tottenham reserves at the Dell. Floodlighting was finally allowed for Cup ties from 1955 and for League games from 1956.

Another technical advance Chapman saw on the Continent was the ten-yard semi-circle to ensure that players kept their distance during a penalty kick. In 1929 he asked permission to introduce the semi-circle at Highbury, but was refused. Four years later the England selection committee saw the semi-circle during their visit to Switzerland and Italy, and wondered why no one had called for its use at home. The new marking was introduced in England in 1937.

Most of Chapman's suggestions ultimately became standard practice, but one of his favourite hobby-horses, although still discussed, has never materialized. This was the introduction of goal judges. It was not a new idea, but in Chapman it found its most ardent champion. In the *Sunday Express* he said that goal judges 'must come' to give more help to referees in avoiding errors of judgement. 'We owe it to the public that our games should be controlled with all the exactness that is possible.' It was ironic in view of this that a hotly-disputed goal was to cost Arsenal the Cup in the 1932 final. For greater control of the game, Chapman also advocated two referees to eliminate the small, unnoticed offences.

The repeated frustration of his attempts to introduce changes led to an impassioned plea in the *Sunday Express* for more freedom of action at club level: 'I appeal to the authorities to release the brake which they seem to delight in jamming on new ideas ... as if wisdom is only to be found in the council chamber. ... I am impatient and intolerant of much that seems to me to be merely negative, if not actually destructive, legislation.'

Not all of his ideas, however, went without immediate reward. In January 1931, after Aston Villa had held Arsenal to a draw in the Cup at Highbury, he decided, for the replay, to make use of new rubber studs to overcome the slipperiness of the icy pitch at Villa Park. The new studded boots gave his players poise and confidence and were a vital factor in their 3–1 win. Nevertheless, rubber studs did not immediately come into general use because the process of changing them ruined the soles of the boots.

Chapman's revolutionary ideas extended also to the running of the national team. During the 1920s and '30s England pursued an isolationist policy, withdrawing from FIFA, the international controlling body, in 1928, and basking in the complacent belief that they were still the supreme soccer power.

Chapman saw the danger signs in the efficient running of such national teams as Austria and Holland. England were beaten by Spain in Madrid in 1929, and in 1932 Austria came to Stamford Bridge and only narrowly lost 4–3. 'We were wrong to laugh at the idea of Europeans mastering football,' said Chapman in the *Sunday Express* after the game. 'Three years ago, when I said British superiority would be challenged, it was said I exaggerated. Now it has come true.' His own rise to fame at club level had demonstrated the superiority of management by one man over management by a group, but the England team was still selected by a dozen officials 'expressing their views as to the merits of players without proper regard to blend and balance'. Selection, he believed, required the expert knowledge of a man close to the players, but the idea of one England team manager was inconceivable even to Chapman. He recommended that the selection committee should be cut to three.

A more revolutionary proposal of his was that England players should train together regularly, an idea derived from his visit to Holland, where the national players came together for coaching once a week, and were given lectures and 'homework' exercises. But he despaired of the idea catching on in England: 'We could never, I fear, get the youths of this country to go to all this trouble to perfect their play.' [5] England training took another twenty years to get organized.

Yet Chapman saw that the future of English football ultimately depended on the young, and he was particularly concerned to win youngsters over to soccer and away from rugby, a concern heightened by the fact that his two sons, Ken and Bruce, were distinguishing themselves in the rugby code. In 1933 a scheme was launched for classes to be held for schoolboys during the autumn term under the management of the Corinthians, the amateur club, with Arsenal as sponsors and Chapman taking classes in basic skills, positional play and training. Professional players were to give practical instruction. Chapman was keen on the plan because he had seen the advances made on the Continent, where such classes were already established. The first team produced by the Arsenal-sponsored scheme did not disappoint, and he urged the introduction of professional coaching into youth clubs and both the public and local authority schools.

'Chapman thought deeply about an infinite variety of subjects associated with the game,' Bob Wall writes. 'He possessed the gift of seeing ahead of his time. He was able to visualize how soccer could benefit from adopting ideas which, in their infancy, seemed to most other people to be merely the outpourings of an eccentric mind.'[6]

Despite his impudent experiments and opinions, Chapman was highly regarded by the FA, which often sought his advice on domestic and international matters.

Nevertheless, he only once travelled with the England party, to Rome in 1933, when he gave the team a tactical talk before their clash with Italy. Apart from meeting Mussolini, he remembered the occasion chiefly for the panic at half-time when he temporarily lost the key to the locked dressing-room. As club manager, however, he was widely travelled and widely respected on the Continent, spreading the name and prestige of Arsenal in his imperialist fashion. Arsenal's main continental venture was the series with Racing Club of Paris, the first game taking place on 11 November, 1930 (when Arsenal won 7–2) at the instigation of Chapman and Jean Bernard-Levy, the Paris club's president. As the fixture was in aid of disabled veterans of the Great War, it was held close to Armistice Day each subsequent year. The series gave Chapman and his players their first experience of air travel, a venture which in the early days of flying took some courage. Alex James and David Jack in particular were reluctant passengers.

Chapman received tokens of esteem from foreign clubs and countries, including a decoration from the French Government and a hand-painted Dresden china service from the Austrian FA. Hugo Meisl described Chapman as 'undoubtedly the leading man in association football throughout the world'. In 1932, amid growing fears that English players would be lured away to foreign shores, the rumour circulated that the Parisians had made an offer for David Jack. It was denied, but a Paris official asked: 'Do you think we could persuade Mr Herbert Chapman to join us? He is the man we would like.'

It could not be long before the football emperor was in truly royal circles. He met King George V, Queen Mary and the Prince of Wales, and often discussed points of play with the King during Cup finals. His prestige received a further boost in the late 1920s when the *Sunday Express* invited 'the famous manager of the Arsenal Football Club' to contribute a weekly column, a degree of journalistic attention unprecedented for a football manager. The column was a popular feature and was revived several times. And it was not only during the football season that the club enjoyed publicity, for the Arsenal cricketers were regular contenders in the London *Evening News* Cup, with Chapman as wicket-keeper.

Although Chapman was by now a famous man, and his name was familiar to thousands who had never attended a football match, on a social level he remained as affable and unassuming as the next man. As a youth, the Reverend A. Hunt Cooke used to sit behind Chapman and his family most Sunday mornings at St Mary's Church, Hendon. 'We used to say good morning to each other and he always smiled at me,' he recalls. 'He seemed a kindly person, not in the least severe. He was just an ordinary, home-loving man, although of course in his profession he was far from ordinary.' Chapman was a sidesman at the church and a good friend of the vicar, the Reverend Norman Boyd, who was a regular guest at Arsenal's home matches.

Chapman was devoted to his family of two sons and two daughters. Asked what was his greatest hour, he replied: 'When my son qualified as a solicitor.'

14

TOP OF THE GREASY POLE

After winning the Cup in 1930, with the forward line of Hulme, Jack, Lambert, James and Bastin the most powerful the game had yet seen, there was every reason to hope for the League title next season. The hope was realized – but in a style that must have exceeded even Chapman's wildest dreams.

Arsenal won their first five matches and did not lose until the tenth. Sheffield Wednesday and Aston Villa challenged hard, but fell away in the spring. Arsenal were home and dry.

New records had been set with almost every triumph Chapman had ever engineered, but none equalled those of Arsenal's 1931 Championship. Not only were Arsenal the first southern club to win the title, but their 66 points were six better than the previous high of Sheffield Wednesday the year before: 28 out of 42 games were won, only four lost, and wins, draws and losses were evenly divided between home and away; the goals total, 127, was one less than Aston Villa's all-time high of the same year. The 66 points were not equalled until thirty years later, when Spurs won the Double, and not surpassed until 1969, when Leeds United made 67.

Top scorer was Jack Lambert, who topped by seven Jimmy Brain's record for the club of 31 goals in 1925-6. The composition of the team remained virtually unchanged throughout the season, and its consistency was proof of the soundness of Chapman's machine. Cliff Bastin's verdict on the season's triumph was unequivocal: 'This Arsenal team of 1930-31 was the finest eleven I ever played in. And, without hesitation, I include in that generalization international teams as well. Never before had there been such a team put out by any club.'[1]

Arsenal's mastery of the First Division was already making

them the best-loved, best-hated club. The critics levelled the
charge that Arsenal's successes were based only on their ability to
buy players, and called them the 'Bank of England' team. They
failed to see that money came from success, not the other way
round – Chelsea, for instance, had also paid large sums for players
without creating a championship team – and that the vital factor
was the genius of the manager in charge for getting the most out
of his players, whatever they cost, and for buying the right man.
Arsenal became the subject of more ill-considered criticism than
any other club, a fate which has more or less persisted.

The practical key to Arsenal's rise was the balance effected
between defence and attack, to meet the new conditions of the
changed offside law. With their in-depth defence the Gunners
could now safely sustain an enemy onslaught and within seconds
send the forwards away to take advantage of the depleted
numbers at the opposition's rear. As Chapman observed:
'Although I do not suggest that the Arsenal go on the defensive
even for tactical purposes, I think it may be said that some of
their best scoring chances have come when they have been driven
back and then have broken away to strike suddenly and swiftly.'
He realized the delicacy of the balance, and so hated to make team
changes. 'When they are necessary I try to arrange that they cause
as little disturbance as possible.'[2] Drastic changes only unsettled
the men, and if the side was not playing well, 'the moderate course
is always the best'.

The essence of Arsenal's style was speed, with intermediate
passing reduced to a minimum and every move subordinated to
the aim of scoring. It lacked the sophistication of a complex build-
up like Tottenham's, say, but for sheer excitement it was unsur-
passed. With Alex James as the pivot picking up clearances from
defence and passing immediately to the front-runners, Arsenal
could have the ball in their opponents' net only seconds after being
packed in their own goal area. As Bernard Joy has observed, 'it was
twentieth century, terse, exciting, spectacular, economic, devastating.'[3] And for an audience badly in need of escape from the misery
of financial crisis and economic depression, at its worst in 1931, it
was an exhilarating spectacle.

Sir Matt Busby, who as a Manchester City player often appeared against what he calls 'the magnificent Arsenal of the early Thirties', describes the key role played by Alex James (whom he knew and idolized as a boy in the Glasgow suburbs of their youth): 'James was the great creator from the middle. From an Arsenal rearguard action the ball would, seemingly inevitably, reach Alex. He would feint and leave two or three opponents sprawling or plodding in his wake before he released the ball, un-erringly, to either the flying Joe Hulme, who would not even have to pause in his flight, or the absolutely devastating Cliff ("Boy") Bastin, who would take a couple of strides and whip the ball into the net. The number of goals created from rearguard beginnings by Alex James were the most significant factor in Arsenal's great-ness.'[4]

Arsenal dominated because of their new tactical formation. The full-backs spread out to mark opposing wingers, instead of inside-forwards as under the old style, while the half-backs marked the inside-forwards instead of wingers. The halves played close in front of the defending centre-half, so the defence formed an 'M' figuration, retreating under attack to build a tight defensive structure. The inside-forwards, James and Jack, held back to fill the gap in midfield, so the forward line formed a 'W'. James's role, in fact, was not unlike that of the attacking centre-halves of the pre-1925 era. Under the new system the centre-half's only occasion for going up-field was to force the attack to make up goals lost. Conversely, the forwards were expected to fall back to help the defence under pressure.

Chapman favoured direct attack. 'The quicker you get to your opponent's goal the less obstacles you find,' was his motto. There was no room for the trick that was merely 'showy'. 'I want the best possible football, but . . . it must be purposeful, it must be effective.' He rejected the customary function of wingers of going down the line and crossing the ball. Instead, he wanted his wingers to beat the defender on the inside and go for goal themselves.

It was not a system that stifled individual skill. There was plenty of that in James's clever footwork and deceptive body swerve, Jack's artistry, Hapgood's neat, precise tackling and Hulme's fast running. But such skill served the team as a whole. Chapman insisted that his players were not slaves to a system, but merely followed the 'fundamental principles of teamwork'.

Having steered Arsenal to a Cup victory and then to a record Championship, Chapman was at the pinnacle of his career. Success, of course, brings new problems and with Arsenal at the top, the next task was to keep them there. Like Disraeli on becoming prime minister, Chapman could say he had climbed to the top of the greasy pole. He knew the danger of backsliding and kept watch on the average age of the team, which he believed should be reduced each season, and on the form of each individual in it. If a player was not performing well the remedy was a spell in the reserves. In Chapman's view, the foundation of Aston Villa's long history of success was their ability to plan ahead and prepare for the departure of key players. He warned against over-dependence on a single player who might be difficult to replace, and was thus well aware of how hard it would be when Alex James retired.

This accounts for the attention he gave to the reserves, or 'spare men' as he liked to call them. At Huddersfield, a strong reserve force had been a vital factor in the Championship run, and Chapman soon set about building a similar force at Arsenal.

As early as April 1927 an Arsenal team containing several reserves won 3–0 at Aston Villa, to end a series of poor results by more regular teams. The reserves won the Combination that year, retaining the championship until 1931. In 1930 they scored 132 goals, five more than the first team in their record Championship year. For the rest of the decade the reserves never fell below third place, and were champions a further five times.

For the 1931-2 season Chapman planned a triumph even greater than those of the preceding two years. The Cup and League Double had eluded the most ambitious clubs ever since Aston Villa became the second club to achieve it in 1897, in a less competitive era. Chapman considered that to win the Double, Arsenal needed to be leading the League by a substantial margin before the Cup came round. But in their determination to score, the team lost the tactical balance that had served so well before.

The forwards kept up persistent pressure, crowding the opposing goalmouth, while wing-halves Jones and John abandoned their defensive positions to join in the attack, leaving the rear exposed. Points were dropped and three defeats over Christmas, which left Arsenal trailing five points behind Everton, made the Double look like something of a pipe dream.

Chapman's response was to inquire after Grimsby marksman Ernie Coleman and Sheffield United's record goal-scorer, Irish international Jimmy Dunne, both possible successors to Lambert.

His overtures were not immediately successful, but a shrewd buy was Oldham's reserve goalkeeper Frank Moss. According to Bob Wall: 'What impressed Chapman even more than the sureness of his hands was Frank's physical courage. He remained utterly fearless throughout his playing career with us, although towards the end of it he was constantly dislocating a shoulder.'[5]

Another journey Chapman made at this time was to Scotland, to watch Neil Dewar of Third Lanark. Because of the growing publicity surrounding his movements, he decided to lose himself in the crowd, going in through the turnstiles and watching the player from the terraces.

In the Cup the amateurs Darwen (11–1), Plymouth Argyle (4–2) and Portsmouth (2–0) were disposed of to give Chapman another clash with his old club Huddersfield, away. He saw it as a tough hurdle, for Huddersfield were still going strong and his knowledge of their methods was matched by their familiarity with Arsenal's. An element of surprise was needed, so Roberts, the 'stopper', was told to join the attack. It worked. Huddersfield were caught out as the red-haired centre-half rushed forward to meet the cross from a corner, and headed Arsenal into the semi-final.

The tie, against Manchester City at Villa Park, was a classic illustration of Chapman's belief that a team can attack for too long. A City onslaught, fed by passes from wing-half Matt Busby, kept Arsenal pinned in defence until, near the end, City launched a final, determined offensive.

Suddenly a clearance found Bastin, who sped up-field to exploit City's depleted defence and join forces with Lambert, the only other red shirt in the opposition's half. After a quick exchange of

passes Bastin scored and the roar of the crowd had hardly sub-
sided when the whistle signalled the end of the match.

Swift attacks like these, combined with the defence-in-depth
system, fed the 'lucky Arsenal' myth, which grew as the Gunners
won game after game after having the smaller share of play. But
luck doesn't win cups and championships – policy does, and if
there was luck, it was just as likely to go against Arsenal, as events
were to show. The 'lucky' tag stuck, however, for years after and
is still used by people ignorant of its origins.

In a fresh effort to secure Jimmy Dunne, Chapman arranged
to go to Sheffield with his chairman and vice-chairman – in secret,
or so he thought. To his amazement, the ticket collector at Euston
wished him success in his mission, and on his arrival at Sheffield
the porter at his hotel pleaded: 'I hope you're not going to take
our Dunne away.' That his quest was common knowledge
astounded and dismayed him. He was shadowed everywhere in
Sheffield, and he looked back on the experience as his most annoy-
ing transfer bid – particularly as it turned out to be one of his rare
failures.

Consolation came when Ernie Coleman finally joined Arsenal
at the end of the season, for a fee of £6,000.

Arsenal were in the final, but Chapman poured cold water on
hopes for the Double. Intense competition made the Double impossible, he said, and to achieve it a club would need a League
lead of at least eight points by the semi-final. (In 1971, Arsenal
won the Double after being six points *behind* leaders Leeds United
at the time of the semi-final.) Arsenal were three points behind
Everton. Chapman may have been seeking to ease the pressure on
his players, but if he did entertain hopes of the Double, they were
dashed when James injured a knee at Upton Park over Easter.
At that stage Arsenal were a point behind Everton, with a match
in hand. The loss of the Scotch wizard had, as Chapman put it,
'an unfortunate influence on the team'; Arsenal did not win
another match before the final and Everton increased their lead
to seven points. In the four games after the final, then played in
April, Arsenal took seven points, but Everton won the title by two
points. Chapman's consolation was that Arsenal had twice beaten

Everton during the season.

With James out of the running for the Cup final against Newcastle, Chapman called up George Male for his first Cup tie. Male
had joined Arsenal in 1929. He had been playing centre-half for
Clapton, alongside Denis Hill-Wood, son of the then Arsenal
chairman, when he got a telegram from Clapton's secretary Harry
Kordell. 'It told me to meet him by the Princess Alice in Forest
Gate,' he recalls. 'When I got there Mr Kordell was with Herbert
Chapman and we went into a Lyons tea shop, where I signed
amateur for Arsenal.

'I continued to play for Clapton and Arsenal, and signed professional in 1930 – on my twentieth birthday. But I still had doubts
about giving up my job at Lloyds insurance firm, so for another
year (they were yearly contracts then) I was allowed to keep the
job, training two nights a week and playing in the reserves. At the
end of the season Chapman called me in and said it was time for
me to decide one way or the other. I decided to go full-time with
Arsenal.' [6]

In the 1932 final Male was at left-half, while Bob John took an
unfamiliar place at outside-right, Bastin moving inside to take
James's place. After eleven minutes it looked as though the changes
would work, when John headed into the net from a centre by
Hulme. Throughout the first half Arsenal had most of the play,
and Newcastle were held, until a cross from Arsenal's goal line
caught out the defenders and United's Allen, unmarked, headed
home. The most controversial goal ever seen at Wembley had
been scored.

Whether the ball was over the line before it was crossed by the
Newcastle inside-right, Richardson, remained a matter for argument for years after. George Male is adamant: 'The ball was
over. I was there. I saw it,' and Chapman backed his players' view:
'I could not see clearly from my position, but Arsenal, almost to a
man, stopped playing and I do not think they would have done
that unless they had been satisfied that the ball had been out of
play,' he told the *Sunday Express*. Photographs later showed that
the ball had been dead before it was centred.

Typically, Chapman did not blame the referee for standing by his decision to allow the goal. At half-time he tried to encourage his players by reshuffling his forwards, but they never regained their form. Another goal by Newcastle completed Arsenal's fall between the two stools of Cup and League, and gave United the distinction of being the first team to win a Cup final after being a goal down. Rumours that the Football Association had ordered a replay made it necessary for secretary Sir Frederick Wall to issue a statement confirming the result.

Chapman made no excuses – 'I say frankly there are none' – and agreed that Newcastle deserved to win because of their superiority in the second half. He could not but point out, however, that James's absence had given Newcastle added confidence. And he defended his players. Asked why Hulme, with an open goal before him, did not move up further to be certain of his target before shooting, he answered that the man on the field did not have as clear a view of the situation around him as did the spectator and was not always aware of how much time he had for his moves.

In view of the circumstances of his team's downfall, perhaps the most ironic touch about the final was that Chapman had said in the *Sunday Express* a week before the game: 'I know nothing of the art of clairvoyance, but I should feel happier if someone would foretell me the vital incident which is almost sure to decide the match. It is usually something trivial, a little human error which is so forgiveable in all the excitement of the occasion, which settles it.'

Despite the double disappointment of 1932 Chapman decided against a large-scale restructuring of the side. True, the team was not getting any younger – the average age was approaching thirty – but the manager was a past master at recharging faltering spirits, and in an emergency there was always the strong reserve force to call on.

Only one major adjustment was needed, to replace the captain, Tom Parker, who was nearing the end of his playing days. Chapman's solution was inspired: to turn wing-half George Male into the new right-back. The full-back partnership of Male and Hapgood flowered into one of the most effective in the history of the game, appearing regularly for England in the 1930s. Tom Parker left to manage Norwich, and in later years became assistant manager of his original club, Southampton. Bob Wall says of him:

'Tom was built in the substantial mould of the pre-war full-backs. He was strong and his resources of stamina enabled him to play just as forcefully in the final ten minutes of a game as in the first ten.

'I think what appealed to everyone about Tom was his utter reliability. Somehow he always seemed to give a thoroughly professional performance – quiet, controlled and extremely efficient.' '

Arsenal started the 1932-3 season as if determined to erase the unhappy memories of the previous spring. A 9–2 win over Sheffield United on Christmas Eve gave them the League leadership. On their way to the top the Gunners, in their new red and white shirts, had given the crowd plenty of thrills, including a classic contest at Villa Park where they were beaten 5–3 after twice being in the lead, and a 3–3 draw at home to Derby in which Roberts twice headed into his own net. But over-confidence took a hold after the leadership was attained, points were dropped, and when Arsenal were drawn away to Walsall, of the Third Division North, in the Cup, Chapman himself fell victim.

With such lowly opposition he saw no cause for worry in the injured Hapgood, the off-form Hulme and the 'flu invalids John, Lambert and Coleman. Unfamiliar names from the reserves appeared in the line-up on 14 January – Tommy Black at left-back, Norman Sidey at left-half, Billy Warnes at outside-right and Charlie Walsh at centre-forward. Only Sidey had ever played in the first team.

To Chapman's horror, Arsenal were a goal down fifteen minutes from the interval, to deafening cheers from the home supporters that could be heard for miles around. The first of the great giant-killing acts was in progress. Arsenal experienced some fierce tackles, but the most crucial came from one of their own men, Tommy Black, who was booked for a foul – in the penalty area. The offence was the result of a bitter feud between Black and a Walsall forward.

As Cliff Bastin later recalled: 'Relations between these two had gradually been becoming more and more strained, until it ulti-

mately came to a point at which the question was which of them
would be the first to vent his feelings on the other. Unfortunately
for us, it was our man.'[8]

The penalty gave Walsall their famous 2–0 win and Chapman,
swallowing his pride, went into their dressing-room after the game
to congratulate them. 'Never have I seen Herbert Chapman look
so miserably unhappy,' says Bastin. 'He made a brave, desperate,
but unavailing effort to cheer us all up. "Never mind, boys," he
said, "these things do happen." But we were all inconsolable, and
so, for that matter, was he. I think he felt the blow more than any
of us. Here was the team which he had come to when it was
struggling pathetically at the bottom of the First Division; the team
which he had made one of the greatest in the history of football,
beaten by a fifth-rate side. Napoleon must have felt like that in
Russia, 120 years before.'[9]

The purge was quick to follow. Chapman set high standards of
behaviour on the field and Black's foul was unforgivable. He was
banned from Highbury, then transferred to Plymouth. Walsh was
transferred to Brentford and Warnes to Norwich. Only Sidey
remained as reserve. It was a reaction reminiscent of that following Huddersfield's stormy League encounter with Notts County
ten years before, when Chapman transferred the suspended Islip.

On the Sunday after the Walsall débacle, Alex James telephoned his manager to offer his condolences. Chapman was
painfully aware that he had underestimated the task at Walsall.
The only consolation was that Newcastle and Sheffield Wednesday, whom he had predicted would still be in the Cup along with
Arsenal, had also fallen at the first hurdle to lesser teams. He put
on a brave face to *Sunday Express* readers: 'I hope it will be
believed that the Arsenal can take a licking as well as any other
club. It is true that it was a dreadful blow, and that we were
bitterly disappointed, but we offer no excuses. There were none.'
Besides, it was not the first disappointment. 'Could anything be
worse than to be beaten in two Cup finals?'

For decades after, Walsall remained the famous name in giant-
killing folklore, a kind of perverse tribute to Arsenal's greatness,
but with other, more recent, spectacular Cup exits, notably that of

Leeds United at the hands of Colchester in 1971, the Walsall ghost may finally have been laid to rest.

Arsenal's poor performances in January 1933 sparked off a minor panic among supporters, and Chapman was even called upon to deny the widespread rumour that the new West Stand was to be dismantled and re-erected at Tottenham, the ultimate ignominy. But the Cup defeat brought out the team's fighting qualities, and a resurgence took them to the League Championship with 58 points, four ahead of Aston Villa, and with 118 goals. At the celebration banquet, Chapman pondered, as ever, on how to keep Arsenal on top, and looked forward to another championship the following year.

THE HIGHBURY FAMILY

The French boxer Georges Carpentier made his name by winning the world heavyweight title in 1914 at the age of twenty. Herbert Chapman saw the key to the boxer's success in the relationship with his manager Descamps, a relationship not of boss and worker, but of partners, combining managerial guidance with sporting skills in a common cause.

Chapman always admired this partnership, based, he believed, on mutual respect and understanding, and liked to view his own position at Highbury in the light of it. For although his authority was supreme, he preferred to regard himself not as a dictator but as a partner, acting together with directors, players and everyone else in the club in a common purpose. He was the first football manager to appreciate the importance of such harmony and to put it into effect. It was a lesson learned from hard experience at other clubs, and one clearly illustrated by Arsenal's own past, in the troubled days before Chapman took over. He believed that 'a club should be like a big family, with all members of it sticking and pulling together under one head'.

His philosophy of management was neatly summed up in his reply when asked what he would do if he were a referee, a prospect he likened to being 'thrown to the lions':

'It is not good that one should seek to display authority by adopting an aggressive attitude. My aim would be to fit myself into the game unobtrusively. . . . But there would never be any doubt about my firmness and authority.'[1]

While he believed that football had grown too complex to be a mere 'director's hobby', Chapman set out to foster harmonious relations at the very top, by acting in a spirit of co-operation with his directors, keeping them fully informed of team matters, and

16 An Arsenal squad leaving for Paris for a match against the Racing Club; Chapman, centre, in plus-fours.

17 On the touchline at the 1932 Cup final: Tom Whittaker, Alex James and Herbert Chapman.

18 Bob John, Herbert Chapman and Alex James on the pitch at Highbury, 1932.

19 The weekly game of golf. *L. to R.*: Tom Parker, David Jack, Herbert Chapman and Alex James.

20 The gym at Highbury. Arsenal players watch new equipment being demonstrated.

taking their suggestions into account. In a later age the policy was taken up at Manchester United by Sir Matt Busby, who wrote: 'Look at the top when analysing clubs who have lasting success and there you will find the original cause of the happy effect. There was never a club with an unhappy chairman and an unhappy board that achieved lasting success at anything.'[2]

With his players, Chapman's aim was to inspire confidence in themselves and a sense of loyalty to the club. The weekly team talks improved their motivation and heightened their involvement, and weekly rounds of golf helped them to relax. 'Get them out golfing and they'll forget all their troubles' was his maxim. He set great store by what he regarded as the dignity of the athlete, treating his players as human beings instead of mere paid servants, which was how most other players were regarded elsewhere.

He wanted footballers to have a respectable place in society, breaking away from their traditional cloth-cap image, and expected his own players to adopt respectable standards of dress and behaviour. They were to be worthy members of the Arsenal family off the field as well as on. Younger players in particular were expected to be clean-living. 'Do you smoke or drink?' was the first question Chapman asked the seventeen-year-old Eddie Hapgood. Even among senior players, outside pursuits were tolerated only so long as they did not affect a player's performance or make football of secondary importance to him. The 'temptations' of the jazz era in London's West End, especially to Cup finalists, were a real danger, and Chapman constantly reminded his players that 'they only count as long as they retain their form on the field'. A source of worry in this respect was Alex James, with his taste for night clubs, but it never seemed to affect his game to any great extent.

Looking to his players' financial welfare, Chapman got the go-ahead from the League to launch a savings scheme whereby £1 or so from each man's wages was kept in the Arsenal 'bank' to earn 6 per cent interest, the scheme covering junior players as well. It was a wise move at a time of economic depression, when a player could earn £8 a week at most in the winter and £6 in summer. The scheme was scrapped when the maximum wage was abolished, in more inflationary times, thirty years later.

Chapman insisted, too, that his players should have decent club conditions, and the Highbury dressing-rooms were rated the best in the country at a time when most clubs were content to provide only the most spartan of facilities for changing and cleaning. George Male remembers:

'I was most impressed with club conditions at Highbury in those days. No detail was overlooked in making changing-rooms clean, comfortable and convenient, especially where players' feet were concerned. For instance, the commonly-used coconut matting got muddy very quickly after a game and was hard to clean. So it was done away with and another material substituted that could be washed down every day. The floor was heated too.

'We noticed the difference when we visited away grounds. Aston Villa's changing-rooms were the next best to Arsenal's, but most others were pretty bad. At Leicester, for instance, the changing benches, bath and lavatory were all in the same room.' [3]

Matching the model club conditions in its advanced thinking was the first-class training headed by Chapman's right-hand man Tom Whittaker. Whittaker, who grew up in Newcastle, joined Arsenal as a wing-half in 1919, later becoming a full-back, but a knee injury while on an FA tour of Australia finished his playing career. He became assistant to Arsenal chief trainer George Hardy, and set about making a special study of anatomy, massage and electrical treatment.

By 1925 Whittaker had become an expert in his field and Chapman was immediately impressed by his knowledge of football injuries. Hardy, in contrast, with his traditional 'sponge and bucket' approach to treatment, was not the man for Chapman, who wanted an up-to-date training and medical department that could deal with injuries quickly and effectively. When, during a home game in February 1927, Hardy shouted from the touchline to a player to move up-field, Chapman chose to regard it as a breach of his authority and arranged for Hardy to move to Tottenham, where a vacancy had conveniently arisen. He called Whittaker to his office the following Monday morning and made him chief trainer, waving aside protests of inexperience and of indignation at Hardy's sacking.

Under Whittaker sports medicine at Highbury acquired a fame that has become something of a tradition. With a combination of every kind of scientific equipment and a psychological 'mind over matter' approach, he got players fit again in a fraction of the time it took other trainers. In the 1930s top personalities from the wider sporting world took their bruises and broken bones to Highbury. And they still do. As Cliff Bastin has said, 'Tom's healing powers were truly phenomenal. People from all walks of life came to Arsenal Stadium for treatment under his magic hands. One was Bernard Gadney, the famous rugby international. He came down to Highbury on crutches, so grave was the extent of his injury. Some of the most eminent surgeons in London had assured him that his playing days were over. He came to Tom as a last, desperate resort. The following year he was captain of the England rugby team. . . .

'Men who, under any other pair of hands, would have remained on the injured list for three or four weeks, Tom would have fit again in three or four days. . . .

'Without Chapman it is more than probable that his great natural gifts would never have achieved realization.'[4]

Chapman said of Whittaker: 'If trainers were transferred like players his fee would be beyond price.' Whittaker got the recognition he deserved when he was invited to accompany the England team to Canada in 1931.

Such was the enthusiasm Tom Whittaker inspired that players willingly trained five days a week, which was not then the fashion. Training was geared more to general fitness than particular skills, and centred on running and skipping to improve speed and stamina. It was not until the 1950s that greater attention was paid to ball control, and weight training was introduced to improve physical strength.

In the 1930s, training at Highbury consisted mainly of laps round the field, with assistant trainer Billy Milne or Tom Whittaker himself looking on – and using the occasion away from the treatment room to have a quiet smoke. But the amount of training was not laid down. As George Male explains: 'Each player knew how much training he was capable of, and did it. After all, it was our job to be fit if we wanted to keep our place in the team. And Tom Whittaker realized that – he didn't have to tell us what to do. If Alex James just ran up and down the pitch a couple of times and said, "Right, that's my lot for today", Whittaker knew the reason he couldn't do any more was because his legs were covered in bruises, as they frequently were. But if anyone wasn't pulling his weight, Herbert Chapman soon got to know about it.' [5]

As well as the basic running, experiments were tried with more mechanical devices. Shortly before the 1927 Cup final, a series of bars with a football tied to them was installed in the St John's College training ground adjacent to the club, so that players could practise kicking at the bars and trapping the ball as it rebounded at awkward angles. It sharpened body swerve, movement and anticipation, and led to an immediate improvement in results. Another new technique was 'head tennis', in which equal sides of six or seven players used their heads as racquets. With Whittaker as trainer, it was no surprise that Arsenal players established a reputation as the fittest in the country.

The only major variation in training was during the first ten days before a new season, when players were not allowed to kick a ball. Instead, to strengthen leg muscles after the long summer break, daily walks along the streets of Islington, dressed in ordinary clothes, were the practice, the distance being increased each day.

To relieve tensions in the week before a Cup tie, players were usually taken to Brighton, where the routine was golf on Monday morning, followed by sea-water baths, more golf, training sessions at Brighton FC's ground and (compulsory) cinema visits in the evenings.

Acutely aware of the sensitivities of his players and the pressures they faced, Chapman's long-standing hatred of barracking from the crowd became even more pronounced at Arsenal. He described criticism of Alex James in his first weeks with the club as 'one of the meanest things I have ever known' because it was made before James had time to adjust to the midfield linking role. This bitter hatred of barracking was reinforced by an incident in his office.

He recalled: 'It was signing on time. A youth came into the office, and I put the form before him to sign. To my amazement he covered his face with his hands and burst into tears. "I'm no use to anyone in football and I had better get out," he said. "The crowd are always getting at me . . . I hope I shall never kick a ball again." Yet, at twenty, he was a player of the highest promise. I knew that he had been barracked at times, but I did not realize that he was so sensitive . . . I persuaded him to re-sign.'[6] After a successful return the crowd again got at the youth and Chapman decided to let him go, 'though it meant sacrificing a player who, I was convinced, had exceptional possibilities of development'.

He proposed that barrackers should be thrown out of the ground if they did not respond to an appeal for fairness over the loud-speaker.

Chapman regarded it as his prerogative to deal with players who were not measuring up, and he could be ruthless if he thought they justified it, as in his treatment of Walsh and Black after the Walsall débacle. On one occasion he called a player into his office, took his hat from the hat-stand and threw it on the floor. 'Call yourself a footballer?' he cried. 'Why, you couldn't even kick that.' And, of course, the player dared not!

Then there was the time Joe Hulme asked if he could stay for the weekend in his native Lancashire after an away match at Bolton. Chapman said it would depend on how well he did on the Saturday. Hulme scored twice in a handsome win and confidently expected his leave to be granted. 'What about the three goals you missed?' was Chapman's response. Hulme didn't get his weekend, and was ordered to train for a third team match the following Wednesday.

Such action was not taken out of spite. Chapman's handling of players was based on a calculated appraisal of each man's tempera-ment, and in Hulme's case he obviously considered that a sharp rebuff and a spell in the third team would boost his determination to improve his game. With another player it could have been different – as it was with George Male:

'We had played Everton away,' Male recalls, 'and were on our way to the station after the game – with a police motorbike escort.

So we didn't have to go all the way to Lime Street, Liverpool, Chapman, with his characteristic attention to such details, had arranged for the train to make a special stop at Edgehill Station, to give us a better chance of getting home the same night.

'As it happened, the kick-off was late – there was no fixed time then – and we were hard-pressed even to get to Edgehill in time for our train home, so in the rush we put our coats on over our playing kit for the journey.

'We made it, and Chapman and I were the last on to the train. Suddenly, as we were boarding, he tugged me by the sleeve and said quietly: "You'd better pull your socks up, or you'll be playing for your place."

'I believe he had been planning that warning for some time. I suppose he thought I was not giving of my best, and as I was known as a rather shy, reserved sort, he had decided that a quiet word at an informal moment would be the best approach. And I think it did me good.' [7]

Chapman's accurate assessment of Male's qualities was shown too when he switched him from wing-half to full-back. He turned on his considerable persuasive powers to convince the player not merely that the full-back position was right for him but that he would be the best full-back in the country.

Similarly, he saw that Bastin should move to outside- from inside-left because there was less danger that the youngster would be knocked about on the wing. But when he called him into his office he didn't mention this as a reason for the change. Instead, he told Bastin he was a natural winger. He 'possessed an almost hypnotic power of convincing. By the time I left his office, I felt as if I had been an established outside-left for years,' Bastin later recalled.[8] 'A shrewd student of character', he would 'treat each person as an individual, possessed of his own peculiar strengths and weaknesses.' In any case, Chapman considered that a player should not regard his position as fixed, believing that 'adaptability should be the aim of every footballer'.

As an example of Chapman's passionate concern for his team's welfare, Bastin tells the story of the coach journey to Leeds Station after the Cup semi-final of 1930. 'Our coach was caught in the

centre of an enormous traffic jam, and it looked as if we would be
lucky to get to the station only an hour or so behind schedule. This
wasn't good enough for Mr Chapman. He stuck his head out of
one of the windows of the coach, and roared protests at the policemen who were desperately trying to cope with the traffic confusion.
He continued to do this at frequent intervals, much to the detri-
ment of his imposing and hitherto impeccable black Homburg hat.

'Eventually, Mr Chapman's efforts brought their reward. Our
coach was escorted through the traffic by a score of motor-cycle
policemen: and we caught our train.' [9]

Although Chapman was, as Carruthers of the *Daily Mail* put it,
'a hard and exacting master', his psychological approach, his
obvious understanding of each player's ability and temperament
and his general good humour earned respect and loyalty. He was
not a 'blustering bully', says Cliff Bastin. 'Chapman, who gave
few words of praise and fewer of blame, inspired awe and respect,
rather than fear. He had complete command of us all.' [10] His
régime would now be regarded as a kind of benevolent pater-
nalism, and most players today would be unlikely to tolerate some
of his harsher reactions. But Chapman's players accepted it, and
the mass unemployment of the 1930s is usually pointed to as an
explanation for this. As Bob Wall has noted:

'This fear of losing one's job manifested itself when the new
contracts were being considered around April 1 each year. At that
time of the season all the players, even the stars, were looking into
the assistant secretary's office almost every day, asking if there was
any news of their contracts. All of them carried an innate fear
of not being offered fresh terms for the following season.' [11]

But perhaps there is a deeper explanation for acceptance of
Chapman's firm rule, one rooted in the social conditions of the
time. As George Male puts it:

'Times were hard for many people. Most of us were brought
up to accept discipline, and to discipline ourselves. We didn't have
much, so we learned to make the most of what we did have, and if a
man was lucky enough to have a job he put everything into it. As
a footballer you had a regular wage and people looked up to you.
No player was going to let that go.' [12]

At a time when a skilled worker earned about £2 a week, a footballer could earn up to £8.

And Male confirms: 'There was certainly big competition for places. I remember playing in a reserve game with six internationals at Coventry before a 25,000 crowd.'

The only player who was prepared to argue with Chapman was Alex James. When he came to Arsenal, James told Chapman in no uncertain terms that he didn't like his plan to make him a scheming inside-forward. He would question aspects of training and tactics, and in May 1931 refused to re-sign. But Chapman accepted that the short, stocky James was one of football's great characters, an outstanding individualist who liked to do things his own way, like living it up at West End night clubs until the early hours. Even on the field he had his own personal trademark – flapping shirt sleeves and long, baggy shorts, which served both as a landmark for his colleagues and to help keep out the cold he felt so badly. And it was the long shorts that allowed him to wear waist-to-ankle underpants during a game without anyone noticing.

Cliff Bastin said of his celebrated partner: 'The first thing that struck me about Alex was his terrific self-confidence. Nobody had greater faith in the qualities of Alex James than Alex James himself – not even Herbert Chapman, and that is saying something.' [13]

And Bob Wall says of him: 'I think he took a mischievous delight in baiting Herbert Chapman. Alex always was something of a rebel at heart. . . . Chapman gave Alex far more lattitude than any other player. He was shrewd enough to appreciate that here was someone who needed to be coaxed, not coerced. . . . Alex loved a verbal fight . . . but he was generally canny enough not to go too far. He knew that, ultimately, he had to toe the official line because, like any other player, he couldn't afford to be put on the dole.' [14]

Chapman himself was not averse to playing a trick or two on his lively player, like the time he arranged a winter 'cruise' for him. James turned up at the docks expecting a luxury liner, only to find a cargo ship and a deck-hand's job waiting for him. When the 'cruise' to Bordeaux was over he was good-humoured enough to laugh at the joke with the rest of Highbury.

Notable among other characters in the Highbury family of the early 1930s were goalkeeper Frank Moss, renowned for his physical courage against charging centre-forwards, Tom Parker with his calm, almost placid professionalism, Eddie Hapgood, the fitness fanatic, the phlegmatic Cliff Bastin and the jocular Joe Hulme. David Jack was not only an elegant inside-forward, he was an elegant man, always impeccably dressed, his main weakness being cigarettes. As writer of a weekly newspaper column, he was allowed his own room in hotels, and from the corridor could be heard above the typewriter coughing away as he smoked one cigarette after another. In his early days at Highbury he was painfully aware of being labelled the first £10,000 footballer. His first game for Arsenal was a nightmare, and before the 1930 Cup final he told Chapman how anxious he was Arsenal should win, so he would justify his record fee. But Chapman said later: 'If we had lost at Wembley, my opinion of Jack and his value to the Arsenal would not have changed in the slightest. I should still have thought that in securing him from Bolton Wanderers I had made the best bargain of my life.' [15]

Many and varied then were the personalities behind Arsenal's phenomenal success, and studying them constantly was the tireless brain of soccer's Napoleon, forever working out how to get the best from each of his players. It was a human approach to football management in stark contrast to conditions beyond the boundaries of Arsenal Stadium. Chapman's mind worked day and night on motivating not only his players but everyone involved with the club, on keeping Arsenal in the public eye, on planning their victories, and on improving the game in general.

It was typical of his thorough approach that after Arsenal won 7–1 at Wolverhampton, he spent nearly two hours at the team talk analysing what led up to Wolves' one goal, much to the dismay of the players, who expected only a brief meeting after such a handsome win. As George Male points out: 'It was done to foil any over-confidence we may have had for the next game, for he knew the opposition would go all out against us after our big win. He reminded us that if we hadn't scored at Wolves we would have lost the game. Today's players would laugh at such a fuss.' [16]

So seriously analytical was Chapman's mind that he would rarely comment on a match until several days later, after he had studied every move. Present Arsenal chairman Denis Hill-Wood says: 'If we asked him after a game what he thought of so-and-so's performance he would say, "Ask me on Monday." He would only give considered opinions. His approach to everything was meticulous, and his decisions were usually the right ones. Even now, Bob Wall and I, when thinking over a problem, ask ourselves, "What would Herbert Chapman have done?" '[17]

Perhaps, as Cliff Bastin remarked, 'He should have been prime minister.'

THE LAST CAMPAIGN

Arsenal, having won the Cup and two Championships in four
years, could not go on for much longer with the same team, and
in 1933 Chapman's major concern was to find replacements to
keep the club on top. As successor to David Jack, he earmarked
Ray Bowden, Plymouth Argyle's stylish winger – on the recom-
mendation of Jack's father, who was still Argyle's manager. At first
Bowden was unwilling to go to London, but he changed his mind
after an assurance that he would be free to return to Devon to
attend to his business affairs when necessary. Chapman caught
the midnight train to Plymouth and the deal was settled. Later he
went to Torquay to sign the speedy winger Ralph Birkett as eventual successor to Hulme.

When the veteran Lambert moved to Fulham in October 1933
Chapman launched a fresh offensive to sign Jimmy Dunne from
Sheffield United. This time he succeeded, and the striker came to
Arsenal for £8,000. The deal was agreed on a Friday night and
Dunne was rushed to London to make his début against Middles-
borough the next day.

Replacements were also needed for wing-halves Jones and John,
and Chapman opened negotiations for Bradford's Jack Crayston,
a long-throw expert, smart dresser and fitness fanatic, and for ex-
miner Wilf Copping of Leeds United.

League performances recovered from early-season reverses to
wrest the leadership from newly-promoted Spurs by the New
Year, Arsenal leading by four points. Despite the chill he caught
on New Year's Day 1934 while watching a game at Bury, Chapman decided to go to Sheffield the next day to watch the Wednesday, Arsenal's next opponents at Highbury. He had studied
closely the threat posed by a reorganized Wednesday side but

insisted that his own presence at Sheffield would be of psychological
value to Arsenal on the Saturday. When he came back from what
was to be his last visit to the city of his youth his high temperature
had worsened and he was advised to rest by the club doctor. But
the reserves were playing next day at Guildford: an opportunity
to see them play was too good to miss. Returning from Guildford
to his Hendon home, he had finally to accept his deteriorating condition. He went to bed, but it was too late – pneumonia had set in.
His family were encouraged by signs of a recovery on Friday, but
at three o'clock the next morning, 6 January, 1934, two weeks
short of his fifty-sixth birthday, Herbert Chapman died.

The news was received at Highbury with shock and disbelief.
No one had realized the seriousness of the illness, and the players
only heard about his death from newspaper billboards on their way
to the ground. George Male was walking to Upton Park tube
station when he saw the bill: 'Herbert Chapman Dead.' 'That was
the first I knew about it,' he recalls. 'I couldn't believe it.' At the
same time, in Huddersfield, Chapman's former colleague Dick
Parker, who had heard that the Arsenal manager was ill, was on
his way to the Leeds Road ground. 'As I turned the corner I saw
the flag flying at half-mast and the meaning of it came like a flash.'

A minute's silence was observed before the afternoon kick-off,
after which a stunned Arsenal managed to hold Wednesday to a
draw.

The funeral four days later befitted an emperor. In cold January
weather a crowd of 2,000, kept on the pavement by a police
cordon, lined the streets to watch the cortège, draped in the
imperial splendour of red and white, move from the Chapmans'
home in Haslemere Avenue to Hendon Parish Church. Cars,
coaches and lorries brought more than 240 wreaths, most in red
and white, many of them from abroad, and some in the shape of
a football pitch. Inside the church was a congregation of 800,
including many representatives from British and foreign football
organizations, but none were more moved than the players and
officials of the club Herbert Chapman had brought to greatness.

The service was conducted by the vicar and Chapman's friend,
the Reverend Norman Boyd, who spoke of the sportsmanship of

this 'outstanding personality of the football world'.

'Football,' he said, 'is a game. And in a game nothing matters so much as the spirit in which it is played. The dangers of professionalism are obvious, and against them Herbert Chapman steadfastly set his face . . . victory can be purchased at too great a price. In standing out for true sportsmanship on the field Mr Chapman, loyally backed by his players, set a standard which has raised the sport he loved to the highest level, and has won for him the gratitude of sportsmen the world over.'

The parish magazine later recorded that the crowds outside the church kept within 'the bounds of reverent remembrance' for the burial, but the Reverend A. Hunt Cooke, Chapman's young acquaintance at St Mary's, remembers the scene as a 'shocking affair'. 'There were people climbing all over the graves with cameras. Mr Chapman would not have approved.'

The magazine, acknowledging Chapman's faithful work at the church, also paid tribute to his character and standing in the football world. 'At St Mary's he will long be remembered for his quiet, firm, and kindly but unassuming manner, apart from his service as a sidesman and his reputation in the country. . . . He was a true friend to sport, and cared no less for the manner in which success was achieved than for success itself. His team played splendid football, as clean as it was clever.'

THE LEGACY

The results he achieved in his lifetime won Chapman universal acclaim, lifting the obscurity surrounding the office of football manager. But a greater tribute to his genius were the results that continued to be achieved after his death by the two clubs he had put on such solid foundations. After completing their Championship hat-trick in 1926 Huddersfield remained a strong League side for another ten years, while making a further three appearances in the Cup final. But it was Arsenal, where Chapman had spent his longest period as manager, who held the limelight in the last years of peace.

'Arsenal always win something' went the saying after they won the Cup for the second time in 1936. The year before they had taken the League title for the third time running, becoming the second, and last, club to do the hat-trick, after a season that saw Highbury's record crowd – 73,295 for the game against Sunderland in March 1935. Director and journalist George Allison kept the honours coming as manager, supported by Tom Whittaker and assistant manager Joe Shaw.

Allison completed negotiations, begun by Chapman, for Crayston and Copping, but his most illustrious buy was Ted Drake from Southampton in May 1934. Dunne, Chapman's last attempt to find a successor to Lambert, proved to be past his best, but Drake more than made up for lost time, scoring 42 League goals in 1934-5, a club record for a single season. His most famous scoring feat was all seven goals in the 7–1 win at Aston Villa in December 1935.

With Alex James continuing in midfield, Arsenal carried all before them, but the day of reckoning came in the summer of 1937 when James retired. The loss of such a man at most other clubs would have spelt disaster, but Chapman had foreseen the danger and the solid foundations he had built at the club enabled Arsenal to win another League Championship the following year. Bryn Jones was bought from Wolves as James's successor in 1938 but war intervened to cut short his career. Tom Whittaker took over as manager after the war, adding two Championships and two Wembley appearances – one successful – to the honours list. He was the last manager with first-hand experience of Chapman's methods and after he died in 1956 there set in the lean period which lasted until 1970. It says much for the resilience of the club, however, that for most of this period a healthy League position was held (lowest finishing place was fourteenth in 1966) and Chapman would be proud to know that, nearly fifty years after his death, Arsenal are the longest surviving member of the First Division.

Arsenal's tours abroad were eagerly awaited on the Continent throughout the 1930s. The series with Racing Club de Paris whetted the appetite for overseas adventures, and Arsenal soon became the most widely known and respected club in the world, a model for emerging soccer nations. The Gunners' services were regularly sought by the England selectors, and between April 1933 and November 1948 the England side for full internationals always included at least one Arsenal man. In November 1934 the record was set when seven Arsenal players were in the side that met Italy at Highbury.

Chapman's influence on the subsequent development of football is all-pervading. Managers are more than ever in the public eye; the scientific approach, in tactics, medical treatment, ground improvements, is commonplace; floodlighting, numbered players, the ten-yard semi-circle are taken for granted. And by creating a successful team in the South, he wrested the dominance of the League from the northern clubs, putting the competition on a more truly national basis. No one man changed football more in this century than the would-be colliery official who drifted by chance into soccer management.

Yet, because of a prevailing conservatism among the sport's administrators, most of these changes took at least twenty years to come about. And though at Arsenal the manager continued in the role of club supremo cast by Chapman, elsewhere – with few exceptions – it was still the directors who had general control. Major Buckley had a colourful career as manager of Wolves in the 1930s, but it was not until Sir Matt Busby's brilliant reign at Manchester United that the commanding role of manager after Chapman's example was firmly taken up outside the bounds of Highbury. Sir Matt writes of the time he became United's manager, in 1945:

'In those days the manager had the title and usually everybody else made the decisions. Directors chipped in with their ideas of picking a team, and niggled when, umpteen people having poked their noses and opinions in, a team emerged and inevitably differed from their several choices.'[1]

More serious was the decline in English football in the years after Chapman's death. Chapman is often condemned as the instigator of this decline: he 'invented' the stopper centre-half, it is said, and so fathered the growth of negative, defensive football. Yet his team could not fairly be described as negative. One of its surviving members, Joe Hulme, wrote in the Arsenal programme in 1974: 'How I long for a return to wingers, all-out attack – and entertainment.' And he condemned destructive, point-saving tactics, the very tactics so mistakenly attributed to his former manager.

The fault lay with other clubs who responded to the devastating effectiveness of Arsenal's attack merely by turning their centre-halves into stoppers, while failing to grasp that a sound defence was only the springboard to attack and not an end in itself. They overlooked the subtle balance effected by the genius of James. But even if they did not, the style demanded players of exceptional calibre – who were becoming increasingly rare – and a manager capable of moulding them into an effective outfit; in this no one measured up to Chapman. The future was glimpsed by Carruthers of the *Daily Mail*, who wrote of Arsenal after their 1933 Championship:

'If it were thought that other clubs would try to copy them, their example might, I am afraid, be unfortunate. There is only one Arsenal today, and I cannot conceive another simply because no other club have players fitted to carry on the same ideas.'

The consequences were indeed unfortunate. Negative football spread as more clubs switched to defensive centre-halves at the expense of attack. Yet Arsenal, accused of being responsible for this perversion of their own style, kept their place among the goal-scoring vanguard despite the tightening of defences everywhere. Former Arsenal players, notably Joe Mercer and, today, Terry Neill, have carried on their taste for forward play into the realms of management.

While English football, bereft of Chapman's innovating spirit, persisted in its negative outlook, Continental countries developed the 'classical' Arsenal style with that enthusiasm Chapman so often warned about. His warnings were not finally heeded until 1953 when England fell to the Hungarians at Wembley.

Once Chapman had gone there was no one with his dynamism and far-sightedness to carry on where he left off. 'It remains to be seen whether or not there will be disciples who will carry on his work of popularizing football, making it attractive to the shilling-paying public,' commented *The Times* in its obituary. It was to be a long time before any disciples appeared to revitalize the game, and even after Busby, Shankly, Clough and others the cry still goes up (not always reasonably) that football is too negative.

Yet Chapman had his answer for the pessimists: if the game was becoming more defensive it was up to managers and players to do something about it. 'Defence has been perfected to a remarkable degree,' he said, 'and I have heard it suggested that through its further development football may be brought to a state of stalemate . . . it will be a sorry reflection on forwards if they have not the intelligence, the inventiveness to devise means by which they can carry their attack to a successful end.' [2]

Huddersfield's Clem Stephenson had the ability to beat the offside trap of the old-style full-backs; that it was possible to beat the stopper Chapman showed by pointing to the example of Robert Gurney.

Gurney, who scored 205 goals in his fourteen years with Sunderland, worked out a way of drawing the centre-half with him while collecting the ball from the wing then suddenly laying it back to the centre for another forward. All that was needed was skill combined with imagination.

'Insufficient regard is paid to the demands of the public. Give them what they want and you will get their support even in these difficult times,' was Chapman's eternal advice, and it still rings true. Times have changed, but they are still difficult. Pull Chapman forward to the 1980s and he would revel in the challenge. For a confidence boost, all he need do would be to look back on his management days at Huddersfield, where the Town scaled the heights in defiance of the most adverse conditions. 'In the face of what they have accomplished, no club should ever despair.' He said that in the early 1930s, and he would say it again today.

POSTSCRIPT

CLIFF BASTIN. Won 21 England caps during his Arsenal career. Still the club's top scorer with 176 goals. When the onset of deafness made it increasingly difficult for him to hear calls from team-mates, he retired in 1947 and took over a pub in Exeter, in his native Devon.

CHARLES BUCHAN. After retiring in 1928, he pursued a career in journalism and broadcasting. Died in 1961, aged 70.

EDDIE HAPGOOD. Played 393 League games for Arsenal and was capped 30 times before joining the RAF at the outbreak of war in 1939. Parted company with Arsenal in bad feeling over a £750 benefit which the club promised but couldn't pay immediately because of debts. Later managed Blackburn, Watford and Bath City. 'Manager of the Year' in 1953. Died in 1973, aged 64.

JOE HULME. Played 333 League games for Arsenal, with 108 goals. Moved to Huddersfield Town and played his last game with them in the 1938 Cup final. Later managed Tottenham Hotspur.

DAVID JACK. Left Arsenal in 1934 after 181 appearances and 112 goals. Managed Southend, Middlesborough and Shelbourne, Dublin. Died in 1958, aged 59.

ALEX JACKSON. Moved from Huddersfield to Chelsea, but left after a dispute to retire from football at the age of 27. Scored 100 goals in 278 League appearances. Killed in car crash in North Africa in 1946, aged 41.

ALEX JAMES. Made 231 appearances for Arsenal, scoring 26 goals. Died in 1953, aged 51.

JACK LAMBERT. Moved to Fulham in 1933 after scoring 109 goals for Arsenal. Killed in a road accident in 1940, aged 37.

GEORGE MALE. Retired as Arsenal player in 1948 but stayed on to work behind the scenes, including work on the youth team and as a scout.

HERBIE ROBERTS. Left Arsenal in 1938 after 297 appearances. Died while home on leave from war service in 1944, aged 39.

CLEM STEPHENSON. Continued to play for Huddersfield until 1929, when he took over as manager. Died in 1961, aged 70.

FRED 'FANNY' WALDEN. Capped twice as Spurs player, in 1914 and 1922. Died in 1949, aged 61.

Appendix 1: Chapman's Cup Teams

NORTHAMPTON TOWN *v.* Newcastle United. Fourth Round, 1911: Thorpe; Britton, Clipston; Manning, Lloyd Davies, Hampson; Walden, Bradshaw, Lessons, Lewis, McDiarmid.

LEEDS CITY *v.* Hull City. West Riding Cup final, 1914: Hogg; Blackman, McQuillan; Law, Hampson, Foley; Bainbridge, Jackson, McCleod, Speirs, Sharpe.

HUDDERSFIELD TOWN *v.* Preston North End. FA Cup final, 1922: Mutch; Wood, Wadsworth; Slade, Wilson, Watson; Richardson, Mann, Islip, Stephenson, Smith.

ARSENAL *v.* Cardiff City. FA Cup final, 1927: Lewis; Parker, Kennedy; Baker, Butler, John; Hulme, Buchan, Brain, Blyth, Hoar.

ARSENAL *v.* Huddersfield Town. FA Cup final, 1930: Preedy; Parker, Hapgood; Baker, Seddon, John; Hulme, Jack, Lambert, James, Bastin.

ARSENAL *v.* Newcastle United. FA Cup final, 1932: Moss; Parker, Hapgood; Jones, Roberts, Male; Hulme, Jack, Lambert, Bastin, John.

NORTHAMPTON TOWN. Southern League, 1909:

P	W	D	L	F	A	Pts
40	25	5	10	90	45	55

LEEDS CITY. Wartime Supplementary Competition, 1916:

P	W	D	L	F	A	Pts
10	7	1	2	21	13	15

LEEDS CITY. Midland Section, 1917:

P	W	D	L	F	A	Pts
30	18	10	2	68	29	46

HUDDERSFIELD TOWN. Football League, 1924:

P	W	D	L	F	A	Pts
42	23	11	8	60	33	57

HUDDERSFIELD TOWN. Football League, 1925:

P	W	D	L	F	A	Pts
42	21	16	5	69	28	58

ARSENAL. Football League, 1931:

P	W	D	L	F	A	Pts
42	28	10	4	127	59	66

ARSENAL. Football League, 1933:

P	W	D	L	F	A	Pts
42	25	8	9	118	61	58

CHAPTER 2

1 Tony Pawson, *100 Years of the FA Cup*, Heinemann, London, 1972.
2 John Graves (ed.), *Herbert Chapman on Football*, Garrick Publishing Co., London, 1934.
3 Quoted in Pawson, op. cit.

CHAPTER 5

1 Charles Buchan, *A Lifetime in Football*, Phoenix House, London, 1955.
2 Graves (ed.), *Herbert Chapman on Football*, op. cit.
3 Interview with Billy Jones.

CHAPTER 9

1 Interview with Dick Parker.

CHAPTER 10

1 Graves (ed.), *Herbert Chapman on Football*, op. cit.
2 Matt Busby, *Soccer at the Top – My Life in Football*, Weidenfeld & Nicolson, London, 1973.
3 Interview with Billy Jones.

CHAPTER 11

1 Bob Wall, *Arsenal from the Heart*, Souvenir Press, London, 1969.
2 Buchan, *A Lifetime in Football*, op. cit.
3 Wall, op. cit.

CHAPTER 12

1 Graves (ed.), *Herbert Chapman on Football*, op. cit.
2 Wall, op. cit.

3 Ibid.

4 Brian Glanville, *Cliff Bastin Remembers*, Ettrick Press, London, 1950.

5 Bernard Joy, 'Alex James', in John Arlott (ed.), *Soccer: The Great Ones*, Pelham Books, London, 1968.

CHAPTER 13

1 Interview with Bob Wall.

2 Interview with George Male.

3 Wall, *Arsenal from the Heart*, op. cit.

4 Graves (ed.), *Herbert Chapman on Football*, op. cit.

5 Ibid.

6 Wall, op. cit.

CHAPTER 14

1 Glanville, *Cliff Bastin Remembers*, op. cit.

2 Graves (ed.), *Herbert Chapman on Football*, op. cit.

3 Joy, op. cit.

4 Busby, op. cit.

5 Wall, op. cit.

6 Interview with George Male.

7 Wall, op. cit.

8 Glanville, *Cliff Bastin Remembers*, op. cit.

9 Ibid.

CHAPTER 15

1 Graves (ed.), *Herbert Chapman on Football*, op. cit.

2 Busby, op. cit.

3 Interview with George Male.

4 Glanville, *Cliff Bastin Remembers*, op. cit.

5 Interview with George Male.

6 Graves (ed.), *Herbert Chapman on Football*, op. cit.

7 Interview with George Male.

8 Glanville, *Cliff Bastin Remembers*, op. cit.

9 Ibid.

10 Ibid.

11 Wall, op. cit.

12 Interview with George Male.

13 Glanville, *Cliff Bastin Remembers*, op. cit.
14 Wall, op. cit.
15 Graves (ed.), *Herbert Chapman on Football*, op. cit.
16 Interview with George Male.
17 Interview with Denis Hill-Wood.

CHAPTER 17
  1 Busby, op. cit.
  2 Graves (ed.), *Herbert Chapman on Football*, op. cit.

Bibliography

BOOKS

Arlott, John (ed.), *Soccer: The Great Ones*, Pelham Books, London, 1968.

Brown, Deryk, *The Arsenal Story*, Arthur Barker, London, 1972.

Buchan, Charles, *A Lifetime in Football*, Phoenix House, London, 1955.

Busby, Matt, *Soccer at the Top – My Life in Football*, Weidenfeld & Nicolson, London, 1973.

Glanville, Brian, *Cliff Bastin Remembers*, Ettrick Press, London, 1950.

Golesworthy, Maurice, *The Encyclopaedia of Association Football*, 12th edition, Robert Hale, London, 1972.

Graves, John (ed.), *Herbert Chapman on Football*, Garrick Publishing Co., London, 1934.

Joy, Bernard, *Forward Arsenal!*, Phoenix House, London, 1952.

Pawson, Tony, *100 Years of the FA Cup*, Heinemann, London, 1972.

Purvis, C. M. and Alcock, C. W., 'Football', in R. N. Serjeantson and W. Ryland D. Adkins (eds), *The Victoria History of the County of Northampton*, Vol. 2, Archibald Constable, London, 1906.

Savidge, Les, *Your Soccer Team and its Management*, Pitman, London, 1973.

Wall, Bob, *Arsenal from the Heart*, Souvenir Press, London, 1972.

NEWSPAPERS

Stalybridge Standard, 13 February, 1897.
Rochdale Times, October-November, 1897.
Grimsby Gazette, March-December, 1898.
Grimsby Times, September 1898 – May 1899.
Swindon Advertiser, May-November, 1899.

154

Sheerness Times, November 1899 – March 1900.

Worksop Guardian, October 1900 – June 1901.

Northampton Daily Chronicle, September 1901 – April 1902; September 1904 – March 1905.

Sheffield Daily Telegraph, September 1902 – March 1903.

Nottingham Daily Express, May 1903 – March 1904.

Tottenham Herald, March 1905 – May 1907.

Northampton Daily Reporter and *Echo*, April 1907 – June 1912.

Northampton Independent, 11 May, 1912.

The Athletic News, 1909-1912; 1913-1915; 1919; 11 May, 1925; 15 June, 1925.

Yorkshire Post, 1912-1919; March 1921.

Yorkshire Evening Post, 1912-1916; 1919.

Yorkshire Evening News, 1912-1919.

Sports Echo, 1913.

The Times, 14 October, 1919; 20 October, 1919; 28 June, 1933; 8 January, 1934.

Huddersfield Examiner, 1920-1921.

Huddersfield Daily Examiner, 1920-1925.

Sporting Chronicle, 15 April, 1925.

Daily Chronicle, 16 May, 1925; 11 June, 1925.

Islington Gazette, 1925-1934.

Daily Mail, 1925-1934.

Daily Express, 1925-1934.

Sunday Express, 1925-1934.

Daily News, 20 April, 1927.

London Evening News, 23 April, 1930.

Daily Telegraph, 8 January, 1934.

158

Dunne, Jimmy, 121, 122, 139, 142

Elland Road, 61, 64, 74-5
England, 8, 9, 29, 99, 101, 102, 113-4,
115, 143, 145
Everton, 76, 89, 121, 122, 133
Exeter City, 103

Fenwick, George, 55
floodlighting, 14, 20-1, 47, 60, 111-2,
143
football, growth of, 20, 21-2, 23, 28-9
Football Association, 20, 21, 22, 53,
54, 60, 63, 65, 67, 70, 79, 84, 85,
94, 109, 111, 112, 115, 124, 130
FA Amateur Cup, 22, 58, 61
FA Charity Shield, 42, 80
FA Cup, 21, 22, 26-7, 29, 32, 48, 51,
55, 66, 75, 83, 100, 101, 107, 111,
112, 125-6, 142, 143; 1922 final, 77-
9; 1927 final, 99-101, 132; 1930
final, 16-18, 137; 1932 final, 113,
122-4
football clubs: formation of, 21; as
limited companies, 35; and players'
union, 53-4; and World War I, 63-
4, 65-6, 67-8
Football League, 22-3, 24, 35, 43-5,
53, 54, 55, 56, 60, 63, 64, 65, 66, 70,
71, 72, 74, 75, 81, 98, 104, 111, 112,
142, 143
Football League Championship, 11,
29, 43, 80, 83-5, 117, 120, 127; First
Division, 12, 30, 75, 91, 143; Second Division, 23, 43, 53, 64, 65, 72,
91, 104; Third Division, 43, 44;
Fourth Division, 44
Foster, Jack, 76-7
Fulham, 43, 51, 59-60, 139

George V, King, 16, 18, 63, 116
Germany, 29, 42
goal judges, 113
golf, 61, 63, 77, 98, 129, 132
Grimsby Town, 10, 24-5, 121
Gurney, Robert, 145

Halliday, David, 104
Hampson, George, 47, 49, 58, 72
Hapgood, Eddie, 99, 102, 119, 124,
125, 129, 137, 147
Hardy, George, 130-1
Harper, Bill, 93, 100

Highbury, 8-9, 12, 13, 39, 59, 91, 96,
100, 106, 108-9, 112, 127, 130, 140
Hill-Wood, Denis, 9, 10, 95, 123, 138
Hill-Wood, Sir Samuel, 9, 94
Holland, 29, 114
Huddersfield Daily Examiner, 76, 79,
82, 83, 84, 86, 87
Huddersfield Town, 7, 9, 10, 11, 12-
13, 14, 59, 68, 74-5, 98, 100, 102,
120, 121, 126, 142, 146; Chapman
appointed to, 74, 75; club conditions at, 77, 86; financial position
of, 74-5, 76, 77, 79; FA Cup finals,
1920: 75; 1922: 77-9; 1930: 16-18;
and Football League, 74, 79-8; and
Football League Championship, 11,
13, 44, 81, 83-4, 85-6, 142; foreign
tours, 76, 80; ground improvements
at, 77, 81, 87; junior team, 76, 80,
84; new players, 75, 81-3, 85, 87,
88-9; reserves, 76-7, 83, 84, 85; style
of play, 87
Hull City, 59, 64, 65, 107
Hulme, Joe, 8, 98, 117, 119, 123, 124,
125, 133, 137, 139, 144, 147
Hunt Cooke, Rev. A., 10, 116, 141

injury treatment, at Northampton,
41; at Arsenal, 130-1
Islip, E., 78, 84, 126
Italy, 8, 29, 113, 115, 143

Jack, David, 8, 83, 101-2, 104, 115,
117, 119, 137
Jackson, Alex, 88-9, 102, 147
Jackson, John, 59
James, Alex, 8, 102-3, 115, 117, 118,
119, 120, 122, 123, 124, 126, 132,
142, 148; character of, 129, 136; and
1930 FA Cup, 17, 104-5; style
of play, 17, 103, 105, 118, 119, 144
John, Bob, 97, 98, 104, 121, 123, 125,
139
Jones, Billy, 10, 46, 86-7
Jones, Bryn, 143
Jones, Charlie, 98, 121, 139
Joy, Bernard, 118

Kingaby, Lawrence, 54
Kiveton Park, 19, 28, 31, 40
Knighton, Leslie, 92
Kordell, Harry, 123